Barcelona Bound: A Travel Guide

Your Handbook to 100+ Must-See Sites and Hidden Gems

in Spain's Most Vibrant City

Melania Cafaro

COPYRIGHT

TABLE OF CONTENTS

COPYRIGHT.. 1

Introduction..8

Welcome to Barcelona...8

History and Geography.....................................10

Chapter One... 12

Essential Information.. 12

Getting to Barcelona.. 12

Getting around Barcelona...............................13

When to visit Barcelona.................................. 14

What to pack for your trip...............................15

Useful Spanish phrases.................................17

Chapter Two.. 18

Top Sights and Attractions.................................. 18

La Sagrada Familia...18

Park Güell... 22

Casa Batlló... 26

The Gothic Quarter... 30

Bucket List of the Gothic Quarter:....................30

La Rambla... 32

La Rambla Bucket List............................... 33

Casa Milà..36

Palau de la Musica Catalana........................... 42

Camp Nou...46

Chapter Three... 49

Hidden Gems and Local Favorites...................... 49

El Born Center for Culture and Memory........... 49

El Poble Sec neighborhood............................. 55

Poble Sec Neighborhood Bucket List:........ 56

Mercat de Sant Antoni.. 57

Sant Antoni Bucket List................................59

Carrer de Blai...60

Bucket List of Must Visit Places on Carrer de Blai 61

Recinto Modernista de Sant Pau........................ 63

Recinto Modernista Bucket List................... 66

The Montjuic Magic Fountain............................68

Montjuïc Mountain Bucket List........................72

Bunkers del Carmel... 73

El Raval.. 77

What to See and Do in El Raval....................... 78

Plaça Felip Neri.. 83

Chapter Four... 85

Culture and Arts..86

Museums.. 86

Museu Picasso.. 86

Highlights and Must-Sees of Museu Picasso.. 87

Palau Nacional..90

Fundació Joan Miró... 93

The Museu d'Història de Barcelona...................98

Museu d'Art Contemporani de Barcelona....... 100

CosmoCaixa - Science Museum.................... 101

Museu del Disseny... 103

Museu Frederic Marès.....................................105

Museu Egipci de Barcelona............................ 107

Art Galleries..108

Galeria Joan Prats..................................108
Fundació Suñol....................................109
The Fundació Joan Miró's Espai 13...............110
ADN Galera..110
N2 Galera...111
Galeria Valid Foto BCN............................111
Architecture......................................112
Cases Godo-Lallana................................112
Palau Montaner....................................112
Casa Planells.....................................114
Mapfre Foundation in Casa Garriga Nogues.. 114
Museum of Catalan Modernism.....................115
Sant Pau Recinte Modernista.......................117
Casa Batllo.......................................118
Casa de les Punxes................................119
La Pedrera..121
Music and theater.................................122
Festivals and events..............................124
Chapter Five.....................................126
Food and Drink....................................126
Local Specialties.................................126
Tapas Bars..128
Restaurants.......................................129
Fine Dining Restaurants...........................129
Budget Friendly Restaurants.....................130
Vegan and Vegetarian Friendly Restaurants..
130
Food markets......................................131
Cooking Classes and Food tours...................132

Chapter Six..**133**

Outdoor Activities...133

Beaches...133

Barceloneta Beach.. 133

Nova Mar.. 135

Playa De Bogatell.. 135

Playa De la Mar Bella..................................... 136

Ocata Beach.. 136

Sant Sebastià Beach...................................... 138

Hiking and Nature parks................................. 139

Montserrat...139

Getting To Montserrat............................... 143

Getting Around Montserrat........................149

Montserrat Bucket List.............................. 150

Where to Stay on Montserrat..........................152

Camping on Montserrat:............................ 152

Parc Natural de la Serra de Collserola........... 154

Collserola Bucket List............................... 157

Parc del Laberint d'Horta................................ 159

Water sports..161

Cycling.. 163

Golfing... 164

Adrenaline Pumping Activities........................ 165

Day Trips and Excursions............................... 166

Girona... 166

Girona Bucket List.....................................167

Tarragona..171

Tarragona Bucket List.....................................172

Sitges..176

Getting to Sitges..................................... 176

Sitges Bucket List.................................... 177

Costa Brava... 184

Getting to Costa Brava............................184

Costa Brava Bucket List............................185

Vilafranca del Penedès.............................. 188

Penedès Bucket List................................ 190

Figueres... 191

Figueres Bucket List............................... 192

Chapter Seven... 193

Practical Matters..................................... 193

Accommodations................................... 193

Luxury Hotels...................................... 194

Boutique Accommodations............................ 194

Budget... 195

Vacation Rentals................................... 195

Vaccinations:......................................195

Visa Prerequisites.................................. 196

Avoiding Long Queues:.............................. 197

General Travel Advice:............................... 197

Money and Tipping................................. 197

Medical Assistance................................. 199

Internet and Telecommunications................... 200

Final Overview of Barcelona's Boroughs..............201

Ciutat Vella (Old City):.............................. 202

Eixample.. 204

Sants-Montjuïc.................................... 206

Les Corts.. 208

Sarrià-Sant Gervasi... 211

Gràcia.. 213

Horta-Guinardó..216

Nou Barris...218

Sant Andreu..221

Sant Martí... 224

Conclusion...228

Introduction

Welcome to Barcelona

Welcome to Barcelona, a city that is brimming with so much energy, beauty, and charm. Barcelona is a city that has everything, from magnificent architecture to delectable cuisine, top-notch museums, and an abundance of outdoor adventure activities. It's a city where it seems like the sun constantly shines, and the streets are filled with the sounds of music, laughing, and conversation.

Picture yourself taking a stroll down the famous, tree-lined pedestrian street known as La Rambla, which runs through the center of the city. People, street entertainers, and merchants selling anything from fresh fruit to handcrafted goods fill the street. The air is filled with the mouth-watering aromas of wonderful Spanish food, luring you to pause and indulge in some tapas or paella.

Or perhaps you're in front of La Sagrada Familia, one of Barcelona's most recognizable landmarks. The unfinished cathedral's soaring spires tower over the city, illuminating the nearby neighborhoods in an uncanny glow. As you look up at this architectural wonder, you can't help but feel amazement and wonder, wondering how such a beautiful creation could exist.

The beaches should also not be overlooked. Some of Europe's most stunning beaches may be found in Barcelona, with golden sands and waves that are as pristine as the eye can see. Barcelona's beaches have something to offer everyone, whether you want to soak up the sun, go swimming, or try out some water sports.

These are just a few illustrations of Barcelona's charm, beauty, and vibrancy. In this travel handbook, we'll examine everything that this exciting city has to offer, including the top spots for shopping, dining, and entertainment. So, whether you're a seasoned tourist or a first-time visitor, get ready to fall in love with Barcelona because it is a city that truly has it all.

Why visit Barcelona?

Barcelona has an abundance of:

- Beautiful structures can be found everywhere, from the Gothic Quarter to Antoni Gaud's modernist creations like the Sagrada Familia and Park Güell.
- Gorgeous beaches with beautiful waters, such as Barceloneta, Mar Bella, and Bogatell, with lots of chances for water sports.
- Barcelona restaurants serve up delectable food and beverages. With an emphasis on fresh ingredients and classic Spanish fares like tapas, paella, and cava, a thriving nightlife with lots of bars, clubs, and music venues to check out.
- Roman, medieval, and contemporary era influences are evident in the rich history and culture, as well as a strong sense of Catalan identity and traditions.

- A thriving urban environment with year-round festivals, markets, and street performers
- Many outdoor pursuits are available, including skiing, golfing, cycling, and hiking, given Barcelona's proximity to both mountains and the sea.
- Nice folks, a warm environment, a strong feeling of community, and a love of life.
- There are direct flights from major cities all over the world and a well-connected public transportation infrastructure, so it is quite accessible.

History and Geography

Spain's northeastern Catalonia area is centered in Barcelona. It is bordered by mountains and undulating hills as it is situated on the Mediterranean coast. Since the Romans founded the city more than 2,000 years ago, it has had a long and diverse history. Barcelona has been molded over the years by a variety of civilizations and influences, including the Visigoths, the Moors, and the Spanish Empire.

The medieval era, when Barcelona emerged as a hub of Mediterranean trade and business, was one of the most important periods in the city's history. The Gothic Quarter, with its congested streets, Gothic cathedrals, and medieval palaces, was developed during this period. Many of these structures can still be seen standing today, offering an insight into the city's past.

Barcelona went through a time of significant growth and modernization in the late 19th and early 20th centuries. The Sagrada Familia, Park Güell, and the Eixample neighborhood with its modernist architecture were all built during this time, along with many other of the city's most recognizable attractions.

Barcelona has long been known as a center of culture and creativity, and numerous well-known authors and artists have made the city their home. Over the years, numerous political and social movements have taken place in the city, which has contributed significantly to the growth of Catalan culture, language, and identity.

With a population of more than 1.6 million people, Barcelona is a vibrant metropolis today. It keeps drawing tourists from all over the world thanks to its magnificent architecture, lovely beaches, rich history and culture, and lively street life.

Chapter One

Essential Information

Getting to Barcelona

There are many ways to get to Barcelona if you're coming from within Europe. Several airlines provide nonstop service from significant cities like London, Paris, Frankfurt, Rome, and Amsterdam. From other regions of Europe, you can also drive or take the train to Barcelona, which can be a beautiful and enjoyable way to travel the continent.

Getting to   Barcelona will require a long-haul journey for people coming from farther away. Flights to Barcelona are available from many major cities, including New York, Los Angeles, Dubai, Tokyo, and Sydney. To get to Barcelona, you might need to connect through a hub city like London, Paris, or Madrid, depending on where you are.

Surf the internet for the greatest offers when making your flight reservations. Search for airlines with reasonable ticket costs and flexible itineraries. To assist you to identify the finest options, you can also use online travel agencies or comparison websites.

You'll need to get from the airport to your lodging once you arrive in Barcelona. Using a taxi or using public transportation is the simplest way to accomplish this. The distance between the Barcelona-El Prat airport and the city center is only 12 kilometers, and frequent buses and trains run between the two locations. If you want to go exploring on your own, you can also rent a car.

Last but not least, make sure you pack correctly for your trip to Barcelona. The city experiences scorching summers and mild winters due to its Mediterranean environment. Bring lots of sunblocks, breathable clothing, and comfortable walking shoes. And, don't forget your camera—Barcelona is a fantastic place to take pictures!.

Getting around Barcelona

Depending on your means of transportation and level of local knowledge, getting around Barcelona can be enjoyable or difficult. For every kind of traveler, there are fortunately numerous possibilities. Here are some pointers for savvily navigating Barcelona's streets:

In the city center, walking is one of the greatest ways to see Barcelona. With many pedestrianized streets and roomy sidewalks, Barcelona is a city that welcomes pedestrians. In addition to being beneficial for your health, walking is a terrific way to experience the city's sights and noises.

Using the public transportation system to go around Barcelona is another fantastic option. You can get to practically any place in the city thanks to the large network of buses, metro lines, and trams. With bilingual announcements and signs, the metro is quick, effective, and simple to use.

You can also rent a bike or a scooter to explore the city if you're feeling more daring. Renting a bike and getting around Barcelona is simple thanks to the city's expanding network of bike lanes and bike-sharing services. There are several rental alternatives for scooters, which are also growing in popularity.

Taxis are easily accessible all across the city for people who would rather use a more conventional means of transportation. Just make sure you only utilize authorized taxis and negotiate the fee before entering.

Finally, don't be afraid to ask for assistance if you're lost or unsure of how to get around. Barcelona is a welcoming city, and many residents are eager to give travelers directions and information.

When to visit Barcelona

The ideal time of year to visit Barcelona may depend on your travel goals. Let's examine the various seasons and what they have to offer in more detail:

Spring (March to May): Springtime in Barcelona is a pleasure to behold. The weather is mild and pleasant, with daily highs and lows between 15°C and 20°C. The streets and parks are lined with vibrant flowers, and the city is in full bloom. The Sant Jordi festival and the Primavera Sound music festival are two of Barcelona's greatest cultural events that take place during this time.

Summer (June–August): Summer is Barcelona's busiest travel period, and for good reason. With an average temperature of roughly 25°C, the weather is warm and sunny. The city comes alive with outdoor events and performances, and the beaches are humming with bustle. But, at this season, be ready for crowds and increased costs.

Autumn (September to November): If you want to avoid the crowds, the fall is an excellent season to visit Barcelona. The temperature is still warm and comfortable, averaging between 17°C and 23°C. As there is less noise in the city, it is simpler to take in the sights without getting overwhelmed.

Winter (December to February): Winter in Barcelona is a lovely time to visit. Despite the cold, with an average temperature of 10°C, the city is brimming with holiday spirit. It's beautiful to view the Christmas markets and lights, and this is a fantastic time to visit the city's indoor attractions, like museums and galleries.

What to pack for your trip

- Pack comfortable shoes that can tolerate a lot of walking because Barcelona is a city that is best explored on foot.

- Lightweight clothes are recommended because Barcelona has warm, sunny weather, especially in the summer. Pack breathable clothing to keep cool and comfortable.
- Don't forget to use sunscreen and sunglasses to shield yourself from the blazing Mediterranean sun. To protect your eyes, bring sunglasses and sunscreen with a high SPF.
- Bring a small bag or backpack to carry your basics, such as a water bottle, map, and sunscreen, as you'll probably be spending a lot of walking and exploring.
- Bring a travel adaptor with you if you are arriving from outside of Europe so that you may charge your electronics.
- Camera or smartphone: Barcelona is a beautiful city with beautiful views and great architecture, so don't forget to pack a camera or smartphone to record all of your memories.
- Although many Barcelona residents understand English, it's always beneficial to know some fundamental Spanish phrases to aid in navigating the city and interacting with locals.

Useful Spanish phrases

In Emergencies:

¡Ayuda! - Help!

Llame a la policía/ambulancia - Call the police/ambulance

¿Dónde está el hospital más cercano? - Where is the nearest hospital?

Asking for Directions:

¿Cómo llego a...? - How do I get to...?

¿Dónde está...? - Where is...?

¿Podría decirme cómo llegar a...? - Could you tell me how to get to...?

Estoy perdido/a - I'm lost.

Ordering Food:

Una mesa para dos, por favor - A table for two, please

¿Qué recomienda? - What do you recommend?

Quisiera una tortilla española - I would like a Spanish omelet

La cuenta, por favor - The bill, please

At the Market:

¿Cuánto cuesta? - How much does it cost?

¿Tiene esto en una talla más grande/más pequeña? - Do you have this in a larger/smaller size?

¿Podría envolverlo para regalo? - Could you wrap it up for a gift?

Gracias - Thank you

Chapter Two

Top Sights and Attractions

La Sagrada Familia

Designed by renowned architect Antoni Gaud, this magnificent basilica is a remarkable example of modernist architecture. Even though it has been under construction for more than a century, the complex features and remarkable design are breathtaking.

You will be awestruck by the grandeur of the Sagrada Família! This monumental church, designed by the legendary architect Antoni Gaudí, is an architectural marvel that has captured the world's imagination. And here's the best part—it's still unfinished!

Immediately you enter the Eixample district of Barcelona, your eyes will be drawn to the Sagrada Família's towering presence.

It's the largest unfinished Catholic church on the planet, and it's absolutely breathtaking. Gaudí's visionary design seamlessly blends elements of Gothic and curvilinear Art Nouveau, resulting in a style that is uniquely captivating.

The construction of the Sagrada Família began way back in 1882, under the guidance of architect Francisco de Paula del Villar. But it was Gaudí who truly transformed the project when he took over as the chief architect in 1883. With his innovative architectural and engineering style, he infused the church with his signature touch, making it a testament to his genius.

Gaudí dedicated the rest of his life to the Sagrada Família, pouring his heart and soul into the project. In fact, he loved it so much that he's buried in the church's crypt. However, when he passed away in 1926, only a fraction of the church was completed.

Despite the challenges, the construction of the Sagrada Família continued through private donations. However, it faced setbacks during the Spanish Civil War when anarchists set fire to the crypt and damaged Gaudí's original plans. Thanks to the dedication of others and the reconstruction of saved materials, the project persevered.

The architectural style of the Sagrada Família is truly a sight to behold. It's been compared to Spanish Late Gothic, Catalan Modernism, and Art Nouveau. But Gaudí took Art Nouveau to new heights, pushing boundaries and creating a masterpiece that goes beyond surface decoration.

To experience the wonder of the Sagrada Família, it's highly recommended to book your tickets online in advance. This ensures a smooth entry and saves you precious time. Visit their website at https://tickets.sagradafamilia.org/en for all the details on booking and additional information.

Make your visit to the Sagrada Família even more incredible with the Sagrada Familia Oficial app! This handy app is your key to unlocking a world of convenience and information during your visit.

Before you even set foot inside this magnificent church, I suggest downloading the app for a seamless experience. With the app, you can effortlessly manage your tickets right from your smartphone. Say goodbye to long queues and hello to hassle-free entry. Simply book your tickets through the app and have them conveniently stored on your device. Easy peasy!

Sagrada Familia Oficial app also offers an audio guide that brings the history and beauty of the church to life. As you explore the different sections, listen to fascinating insights and stories that enhance your understanding of this architectural wonder. It's like having your own personal tour guide right in your pocket!

And if you're curious about the latest news and updates about the Sagrada Família, the app has got you covered. Stay informed about upcoming events, exhibitions, and special promotions that you won't want to miss.

For the ultimate Sagrada Família experience, I highly recommend visiting in the morning when it opens its doors at 9 am. This is the best time to beat the crowds and immerse yourself in the beauty of this iconic Basilica, which happens to be the most visited monument in Spain. Trust me, you don't want to miss out on this!

- Opening Hours

The Sagrada Família Barcelona welcomes visitors every day of the week from 9 am to 6 pm. However, do keep in mind that on 25 and 26 December, as well as 1 and 6 January, the opening hours are slightly shorter, from 9 am to 2 pm. So plan your visit accordingly.

When it comes to exploring the Sagrada Família, you can expect to spend about 2 hours to fully soak in all its wonders. This includes exploring the towers, visiting the museum located near the crypt, and browsing the store for some souvenirs. And here's a fantastic tip: once you're inside the basilica, you can take your time and stay for as long as you like. So no need to rush!

If you're interested in attending a mass at the Sagrada Família, they hold a special service every Sunday morning at 9 am. It's an international mass, conducted in multiple languages, and lasts about one hour. Best of all, it's free of charge! Just make sure to arrive early, around 8 am, to secure a seat.

- Tickets

Now, let's talk about admission fees. Children under 11 years old can enter for free, but at least one adult ticket must be purchased alongside their entry. And guess what? If you're a disabled person, you and your carer get free entry as well. Just remember to bring proof of your disability.

For young people between 11 and 30 years old, the Sagrada Família offers a special half-price entry during certain periods of the year. You can get this discounted ticket for only 7 euros, but please note that it's only available at the ticket office on Wednesdays, Thursdays, and Sundays between 4 pm and 6 pm.

Park Güell

This is another of Gaudí's works, and it is a fanciful wonderland filled with vibrant mosaics, twisted sculptures, and breathtaking vistas of the city. It's the ideal setting for exploring and losing yourself in Barcelona's allure.

22

Park Güell is a captivating oasis nestled on Carmel Hill in the vibrant city! This privatized park is a true testament to the artistic genius of Antoni Gaudí, the iconic face of Catalan modernism.

Wander through Park Güell, you'll be entranced by Gaudí's unparalleled creativity and his seamless integration of organic shapes into his architectural masterpieces. This park, designed during Gaudí's naturalist phase in the early 20th century, showcases his innovative structural solutions and his unique artistic style.

Imagine strolling through lush gardens and encountering the mesmerizing multicolored mosaic salamander, affectionately known as "el drac," guarding the main entrance. It's a sight that will leave you awe-inspired and eager to explore further.

One of the highlights of Park Güell is the serpentine bench, an architectural marvel that offers not only a place to rest but also a private space for conversation. Gaudí's meticulous attention to detail is evident in the bench's tiled design, cleverly constructed to dry quickly after rain showers. You'll also discover hidden bird nests nestled within the terrace walls, mimicking the trees that surround them.

As you meander along the park's roadways, you'll be amazed by how seamlessly they blend into the natural landscape. Gaudí's use of local stone and his incorporation of natural forms create a harmonious integration with the environment. The roadway structures jutting out from the hillside and the viaducts with footpaths running underneath are a testament to Gaudí's visionary approach.

At the park's highest point, you'll find "El Turó de les Tres Creus," also known as Calvary. This stone hill adorned with three large crosses offers a breathtaking panoramic view of Barcelona. From here, you can marvel at the city's iconic landmarks, such as the Sagrada Família and the Montjuïc area, while taking in the beauty of the bay.

Park Güell is not only a haven for architectural marvels but also a sanctuary for wildlife. Keep an eye out for the colorful parrots that have made this park their home, adding a touch of exotic charm to the surroundings. You may even spot other bird species, such as the short-toed eagle, gracefully soaring above.

To visit Park Güell, you can access it by underground railway, city buses, or commercial tourist buses. Please note that since October 2013, there is an entrance fee to access the Monumental Zone, which includes the main entrance, terrace, viaducts, and areas with mosaics. However, the experience is well worth it, and limited tickets are available.

Make sure to explore Gaudí's house, "la Torre Rosa," which showcases his remarkable furniture designs. And if you're also planning to visit the Sagrada Família Church, a reduced rate is available for combined tickets.

- Some Highlights:

First, at the main entrance, you'll encounter Gaudí's famous multicolored mosaic salamander, affectionately referred to as "el drac" or "the dragon." This iconic sculpture has been lovingly restored after an unfortunate act of vandalism in February 2007. It's a true testament to Gaudí's unique vision and his mastery of mosaic work.

As you explore the main terrace, you'll be captivated by Gaudí's mosaic creations. The intricate and vibrant patterns will transport you into a world of color and beauty. Take your time to admire the meticulous craftsmanship and the way Gaudí's mosaic work harmonizes with the natural surroundings. Don't miss the Porter's Lodge pavilion at the park's entrance. Its roof, adorned with trencadís tiles, showcases Gaudí's signature style. The pavilion is a charming structure that adds to the whimsical atmosphere of the park.

Near the entrance, you'll also find a captivating fountain featuring a dragon motif. This enchanting fountain is another manifestation of Gaudí's creative genius and attention to detail.

Inside the park, make sure to visit the Hypostyle Room, where you'll be greeted by a ceiling adorned with a stunning mosaic. The intricate patterns and colors create a mesmerizing visual experience, showcasing Gaudí's mastery of his craft.

Lastly, don't forget to traverse the three viaducts that span the park. Originally designed by Gaudí to facilitate the transportation of visitors, these architectural marvels continue to serve as pathways, allowing you to explore the park's various sections with ease. They blend seamlessly with the landscape and exemplify Gaudí's innovative approach to design.

These highlights are just a glimpse into the wonder and artistry that awaits you at Park Güell.

Casa Batlló

With its undulating roof, vivid tiles, and curved balconies, Casa Batlló is a magical structure that is frequently compared to something out of a fairy tale. Learn more about the past and creation of this stunning building by taking a tour.

Let's dive into the captivating world of Casa Batlló, an architectural marvel in the heart of Barcelona. Designed by the visionary Antoni Gaudí, this building stands as one of his greatest masterpieces. Originally a house that underwent a remodel, Gaudí took charge of its redesign in 1904, with contributions from his talented assistants Domènec Sugrañes i Gras, Josep Canaleta, and Joan Rubió.

Locally known as Casa dels ossos or House of Bones, Casa Batlló exhibits a unique, organic quality that evokes a visceral and skeletal sensation. Situated on the renowned Passeig de Gràcia in the Eixample district, it is part of the Illa de la Discòrdia, a collection of four buildings by prominent Modernista architects of Barcelona.

True to Gaudí's distinctive style, Casa Batlló defies categorization and can only be described as Modernisme in the broadest sense. The ground floor is a sight to behold, featuring unconventional tracery, irregular oval windows, and flowing sculpted stone work. Straight lines are virtually absent, replaced instead by a vibrant and colorful mosaic of broken ceramic tiles known as trencadís that adorns much of the façade. The roof, with its graceful arches, has been likened to the back of a dragon or dinosaur, invoking a sense of wonder and imagination.

One intriguing theory about the building suggests that the rounded feature to the left of center, culminating in a turret and cross, symbolizes the lance of Saint George, the patron saint of Catalonia and Gaudí's homeland, piercing the back of the dragon.

Recognizing its immense cultural value, Casa Batlló was designated as a UNESCO World Heritage Site in 2005, joining the ranks of Antoni Gaudí's other remarkable works.

Among the many highlights of Casa Batlló, the noble floor stands out with its exquisite details and grandeur. The chimneys of the building are another remarkable feature, designed not only for function but also to prevent backdrafts.

The rooftop of Casa Batlló is a beloved attraction, capvating visitors with its iconic dragon back design. Gaudí's ingenuity is evident in the representation of an animal's spine using tiles of different colors. Additionally, the rooftop boasts four intricately designed chimney stacks.

Other notable highlights of Casa Batlló include the mesmerizing blue lightwell, the elegant catenary arcs, the intricate façade up close, the inviting atrium, and the captivating stained glass windows.

- Online and Ticket Office Discounts:

Adults: Secure your spot for an immersive experience with tickets starting from just €29.

Children (Up to 12 years old, accompanied by an adult): Enjoy free admission and introduce your little ones to Casa Batlló. .

Teenagers (Between 13 and 17 years old): Grab a discounted ticket for only €6. It's the perfect opportunity for young art enthusiasts.

Students (with valid student card from any country): Avail yourself of the special student discount of €6 and discover the artistry of Casa Batlló on a budget.

Seniors (From 65 years old): Enjoy a reduced rate of €3.

Visitors with a card certifying the degree of disability: Benefit from a discounted ticket of €6.

Companions of disabled persons: Enjoy free admission as a companion of a disabled person and share the joy of exploring.

- Additional Discounts at the Ticket Office:

When purchasing tickets at the museum's ticket office, certain cards can grant you exclusive features and discounts. Here are some of the cards that offer special benefits:

ICOM and ICOMOS cards: Enjoy free admission with your ICOM or ICOMOS card.

Barcelona PressCard: Get complimentary access to the museum with your Barcelona PressCard.

Press card: Benefit from a 50% discount off the regular ticket price with your press card.

Carnet Club Super3: Enjoy free admission with your Carnet Club Super3.

Carnet Jove: Avail yourself of a discounted ticket for only €3 with your Carnet Jove.

Usuarios Bus Turístic: Enjoy a reduced rate of €7 as a Usuarios Bus Turístic customer.

Barcelona City Tours customers: Benefit from a discounted ticket price of €7 as a Barcelona City Tours customer.

Barcelona Card customers: Get a special rate of €7 as a Barcelona Card customer.

Barcelona Pass customers: Avail yourself of a discounted ticket for only €7 as a Barcelona Pass customer.

Minicards customers: Enjoy a reduced rate of €7 as a Minicards customer.

Ruta del Modernisme customers: Benefit from a discounted ticket price of €7 as a Ruta del Modernisme customer.

Barcelona Walking Tours customers: Avail yourself of a discounted ticket for only €7 as a Barcelona Walking Tours customer.

Please note that these offers may be subject to change, so it's always a good idea to check the official museum website or contact the ticket office for the most up-to-date information.

The Gothic Quarter

Barcelona's oldest district is a maze of winding alleyways, historic structures, and obscure squares. Discover hidden cafes, artisan stores, and breathtaking Gothic architecture by exploring the meandering lanes.

The Gothic Quarter, also known as Barri Gòtic, stretches from La Rambla to Via Laietana, offering a glimpse into Barcelona's rich history. It's a labyrinth of narrow streets and squares, filled with medieval landmarks and remnants of the city's Roman wall.

Bucket List of the Gothic Quarter:

- Marvel at the Temple of Augustus:

Uncover the secrets of the Roman era at this hidden gem. Tucked away in Carrer del Paradís, the Temple of Augustus is a testament to Barcelona's ancient past.

- Visit Barcelona Cathedral:

Step into the awe-inspiring Gothic Cathedral, also known as the Cathedral of the Holy Cross and Saint Eulalia. Admire the stunning architecture, including the enchanting cloister and the roof adorned with an array of mythical gargoyles.

- Immerse Yourself in History at Santa Maria del Pi:

Explore the exquisite Gothic Church of Santa Maria del Pi, located on Plaça del Pi. Its intricate details and serene atmosphere make it a must-visit spot.

- Experience Plaça de Sant Jaume:

Discover the beating heart of Barcelona's administrative center. This square houses the Palace of the Generalitat of Catalonia and the City Hall, offering a glimpse into the city's governance.

- Stroll Along Portal de l'Àngel:

Wander down the bustling pedestrian street, Portal de l'Àngel, and indulge in a shopping spree. Explore the array of big-name brands and charming independent shops that line this vibrant avenue.

- Uncover Ancient Remains:

Seek out the Roman tombs in Plaça de la Vila de Madrid and the aqueduct in Plaça Nova. These remnants provide a fascinating glimpse into the city's past.

- Learn About Barcelona's Jewish Past:

Explore El Call, the old Jewish Quarter, known for its narrow streets and dark medieval history. Visit the old synagogue and immerse yourself in this unique corner of the Gothic Quarter.

- Discover Gaudi's Early Work:

Admire Gaudi's artistic influence in Plaça Reial, where his street lamps still grace the square. Witness the beginning of his extraordinary architectural legacy.

- Dine at Can Culleretes:

Treat yourself to a culinary journey at the oldest restaurant in Barcelona. With its traditional Catalan and Spanish dishes, Can Culleretes will transport you back in time.

- Experience La Boqueria Market:

Venture to the nearby La Boqueria, one of Europe's oldest markets. Immerse yourself in the vibrant atmosphere, indulge in delicious tapas, and soak up the bustling energy.

- Explore the Gothic Cathedral:

Don't miss the grand Gothic Cathedral, an architectural marvel that took centuries to complete. Marvel at its intricate details and explore the beautiful patios and cloisters.

La Rambla

A popular tourist destination, but for good cause. It's the ideal area to experience Barcelona's vibrancy and ambiance because it is lined with bustling cafes, flower stands, and street entertainers.

La Rambla is a 1.2km boulevard that kicks off at Plaça de Catalunya and takes you all the way to the impressive statue of Christopher Columbus by the port. These days, you won't find any caged animals being sold along the street (thankfully, that was banned in 2006), but you'll notice something interesting: different sections of La Rambla are named after saints. For example, there's Santa Mònica and Sant Josep, whose stretch is even known as La Rambla dels Flors, a nod to the time when churches and convents lined the street between the 16th and 18th centuries. While those religious buildings are no longer standing, fear not! Just a short walk away, you'll discover the awe-inspiring Barcelona Cathedral, with its breathtaking neo-Gothic facade and whimsical rooftop gargoyles.

La Rambla Bucket List

- Dive into La Boqueria Market

Immerse yourself in the vibrant colors and aromas of La Boqueria, Barcelona's most flamboyant market. From local produce to exotic delicacies, this bustling market offers a culinary adventure like no other.

- Admire La Rambla dels Flors

Follow the trail of centuries-old tradition as flower-sellers add a splash of color to La Rambla. Their vibrant blooms have inspired artists, writers, and musicians, making them an integral part of the street's heritage.

- Indulge in Culture at Liceu Opera House

Break free from preconceptions and enjoy an evening of opera or ballet at the Gran Teatre del Liceu. This majestic venue also hosts concerts, showcasing a range of musical genres.

- Visit the Columbus Monument

Expand your La Rambla adventure at the top by ascending the Columbus Monument. Take in the breathtaking panoramic views of Barcelona, including the Gothic Quarter, Raval, and the sparkling Mediterranean.

- Unwind at Cafè de l'Òpera

Step back in time at Cafè de l'Òpera, a historical café with stained-glass windows reminiscent of old Viennese coffeehouses. Savor a cup of quality coffee or indulge in chocolate with churros while people-watching on the terrace.

- Seek Good Fortune at Canaletes Fountain

Quench your thirst at Canaletes Fountain, where legend has it that a drink guarantees your return to Barcelona. With a rich history dating back to the 15th century, this fountain is steeped in local lore.

- Discover Miró Mosaic

Pause and appreciate the enormous mosaic by renowned artist Joan Miró. Its circular shape, primary colors, and distinctive lines add a touch of artistic flair to the pavement beneath your feet.

- Pay Tribute at the 2017 Terrorist Attack Memorial

Take a moment of reflection and pay respects to the victims of the tragic terrorist attack. The memorial, near the Joan Miró mosaic, bears a heartfelt message of peace in multiple languages.

- Delight in Escribà

Treat yourself to delicate pastries and exquisite cakes at Escribà. This patisserie, housed in a modernista shopfront, offers a perfect start to your day, complemented by morning coffee on their terrace.

- Explore Museu de Cera

Step into the quirky world of the Museu de Cera, Barcelona's own wax museum. Encounter famous figures from the past, including film stars, politicians, and historical characters, all immortalized in wax.

- Immerse in Art at La Virreina Centre de la Imatge

Admire the architecture and sculptures at La Virreina, an 18th-century palace turned art center. Explore the free exhibitions featuring photography, paintings, and moving images.

- Taste Galician Cuisine at Centro Galego de Barcelona

Embark on a gastronomic adventure at Centro Galego de Barcelona, where you can savor fantastic Galician cooking at reasonable prices. This hidden gem within a magnificent apartment offers an authentic dining experience.

- Uncover the Erotic Side at Museu de l'Erotica

Embark on an unconventional journey through history at the Museu de l'Erotica. Learn about the cultural perspectives on eroticism, spanning from ancient Roman times to the early 20th century.

- Find Musical Treasures at Casa Beethoven

Discover the Antiga Casa Figueras, transformed into Casa Beethoven, a musical treasure trove since 1880. Whether you're seeking sheet music or a unique gift for music enthusiasts, this shop has it all.

- Enjoy Performances at Poliorama Theatre

Catch a performance at Poliorama Theatre, housed in a building with a rich history that once served as a cinema. From concerts to flamenco shows, this theater offers entertainment for all.

- Engage with Art at Arts Santa Mònica

Drop by Arts Santa Mònica for a diverse range of exhibitions encompassing various disciplines, from visual arts to music and design. You never know what captivating artwork or creative projects await you.

Casa Milà

Casa Milà is another one of Gaudi's magnificent structures. Any lover of architecture must see it to appreciate the sculptures on the rooftop and the building's curved exterior.

Casa Milà, also known as La Pedrera is a remarkable architectural masterpiece located on Paseo de Gracia. While you can admire the facade without an entrance ticket, you'd be missing out on the most fascinating parts if you don't venture inside.

As you step into Casa Milà, you'll have the opportunity to visit one of the nine furnished apartments, explore exhibits like the Espai Gaudí showcasing the architect's work, wander through the inner patios, and marvel at the spectacular rooftop adorned with sculpted chimneys and towers.

The facade of Casa Milà is a sight to behold, rising eight stories with its massive blocks of carved brown limestone. Its smooth, curved forms are said to evoke the sea, while the stone pillars supporting the front of the building allow ample natural light to brighten the interior through numerous windows.

Despite the initial negative reaction to Gaudí's extravagant style, Casa Milà gradually gained appreciation over the years. Locals playfully referred to it as "La Pedrera" (The Quarry) due to its unconventional appearance. Today, you can step inside and get a glimpse into the lives of Barcelona's affluent bourgeoisie from the early 20th century. The interior of Casa Milà has been meticulously preserved, featuring furniture, ornaments, and pieces designed by Gaudí himself, providing a captivating experience.

Two large patios within La Pedrera demonstrate Gaudí's innovative approach, consolidating the small ventilation shafts into these spaces to enhance lighting and ventilation. The walls of these patios are adorned with stunning shapes, lights, and colors, thanks to the multitude of windows and decorative wall paintings featuring floral motifs that mirror those found throughout the entrance halls and stairways.

The rooftop terrace of Casa Milà is a true highlight, boasting 28 chimneys, towers, and spires. Gaudí's signature trencadís mosaic technique, created with shattered pieces of colorful tiles, adorns the rooftop. Look out for the dark green ornamentation made from fragments of green glass sourced from cava bottles. The rooftop also offers spectacular views of Barcelona, and you might spot a heart-shaped element pointing towards Reus, Gaudí's birthplace, as well as a heart and a tear pointing towards La Sagrada Família, symbolizing the architect's poignant awareness that he would never see his beloved church completed.

Within La Pedrera, you'll find the Espai Gaudí, an attic space that houses the only exhibition dedicated to Gaudí's life and work. It showcases models, building plans, objects, designs, photos, and videos, providing a comprehensive overview of the architect's legacy.

The first floor of Casa Milà serves as an exhibition space and offers a glimpse into the apartment once occupied by the Milà family, the original owners. Richly decorated with paintings, including Gaudí's characteristic trencadís, this space often hosts public exhibits.

After your visit, make a stop at Café La Pedrera on the first floor for a refreshing coffee and a bite to eat. You can also explore the gift shop and book shop, where you'll find interesting souvenirs and gifts.

Casa Milà's history and architecture are fascinating. Pere Milà, a local developer, commissioned Antoni Gaudí to build the house. While there were rumors that Pere married Roser Segimon i Artells, a wealthy widow, for her fortune, he was genuinely impressed by Gaudí's flamboyant Casa Batlló nearby. Gaudí received complete creative freedom and a blank check, but conflicts arose between him and Pere, leading Gaudí to abandon the project before its completion.

Gaudí's work faced criticism and was deemed odd and strange during his lifetime. When Casa Milà was finished in 1912, negative backlash ensued as locals feared its unconventional appearance would devalue neighboring properties. A clash between Gaudí and Pere occurred over religious symbolism, resulting in Gaudí's departure from the project. Casa Milà was completed without him, and he devoted himself entirely to the construction of the Sagrada Família.

Public opinion eventually changed, and Casa Milà, along with Gaudí's other renowned works, was recognized as a UNESCO Cultural World Heritage site in 1984. Subsequent renovations and investments transformed the building into a modern tourist attraction, elevating its status and public perception.

If you're torn between visiting Casa Milà or Casa Batlló, we recommend exploring Casa Milà. While Casa Batlló may appear more spectacular from the outside, Casa Milà offers a more captivating interior experience.

As you immerse yourself in Casa Milà's rich history, keep in mind that people still reside within the building, adding a unique dimension to its living legacy.

Casa Milà is conveniently located near two other notable Gaudí landmarks: the Sagrada Família and the Casa Batlló. So, you can easily plan a comprehensive Gaudí tour during your visit to Barcelona.

It is one of the two houses designed by Antoni Gaudí on Passeig de Gràcia, the other being Casa Batlló.

Commissioned by Roser Segimon and her husband Pere Milà, prominent figures in Barcelona's social and business circles, Casa Milà's unique facade constructed entirely of natural stone earned it the nickname "La Pedrera" (The Quarry).

While initially mocked for its unconventional style, Casa Milà eventually gained appreciation and became the iconic symbol it is today.

When visiting Casa Milà, don't miss the breathtaking rooftop terrace, where you can learn about Gaudí's techniques and style. The building has even served as a filming location for numerous movies. Additionally, be sure to catch the captivating evening show called "The Origins" for a truly unique experience.

As a UNESCO Cultural World Heritage site, Casa Milà offers a vast exploration opportunity. Though you won't see the entire building, expect to spend up to two hours discovering its various areas.

Make a point to visit the Espai Gaudí, which provides insights into the architect's process and philosophy.

For the best experience, consider visiting Casa Milà on weekdays, early in the morning, or close to closing time to avoid large crowds. Keep in mind that it can get hot on the roof terrace during the middle of the day in the summer months.

Alternatively, you can opt for a night tour of La Pedrera, which offers a spectacular view from the rooftop at night, accompanied by a light show and a glass of cava.

To save time and avoid long queues, it's advisable to purchase tickets online in advance. Various ticket options are available, including those with audio guides. Discounts are available for children, students, and seniors. Children under 7 can enter for free.

Casa Milà's opening hours are from 9 am to 6:30 pm during the daytime. Nighttime opening hours vary depending on the season. Be sure to check the time slots when booking your tickets.

- Getting There

Reaching Casa Milà is convenient via the metro, with the closest stop being Diagonal on the L3 (green line) and L5 (blue line). Walking from the Plaza Catalunya area takes approximately 15 minutes along Passeig de Gràcia, or you can easily cycle there using the cycling lanes. The Hop-on Hop-off bus (Bus Turístic) also stops right in front of La Pedrera on both the northern and southern lines.

Palau de la Musica Catalana

This spectacular concert hall delights the senses with its exquisite carvings, brilliant chandeliers, and intricate stained glass. The Palau de la Música Catalana, also known as the Palace of Catalan Music, is hands down the most breathtaking concert hall I have ever seen. Not only is it a visual masterpiece, but it is also recognized as a UNESCO World Heritage site. Constructed between 1905 and 1908 for the Orfeó Català, a choral society founded in 1891, this magnificent music auditorium is located in Barcelona, Spain.

Designed by the renowned architect Lluís Domènech i Montaner, a prominent figure of Catalan modernism, the Palau de la Música Catalana boasts remarkable acoustics and is adorned with exquisite stained glass, mosaics, ceramics, sculptures, murals, and wrought iron elements.

Let's delve into a brief history of this remarkable architectural gem. After the establishment of the Orfeó Català in 1891, conductors and composers Lluís Millet and Amadeo Vives enlisted the services of Lluís Domènech i Montaner to create a modernist building that would serve as the society's headquarters. Domènech i Montaner was already renowned for his work on the Hospital de la Santa Creu i Sant Pau, another UNESCO World Heritage site, and was considered one of the leading figures of Catalan modernism alongside Antoni Gaudí and Josep Puig i Cadafalch.

After less than three years of construction, the Palau de la Música Catalana opened its doors to the public. Since then, it has hosted symphonic concerts, instrumental recitals, and performances by world-renowned conductors and musicians such as Richard Strauss, Pau Casals, Igor Stravinsky, Arthur Rubinstein, Herbert von Karajan, Leonard Bernstein, Montserrat Caballé, Claudio Abbado, Daniel Barenboim, and Josep Carreras. The stage has also witnessed the presence of esteemed orchestras and choirs, including the Wiener Philharmoniker, New York Philharmonic, Berliner Philharmoniker, Koninklijk Concertgebouworkest, Chicago Symphony Orchestra, Escolanía de Montserrat, Cappella Musicale Pontificia, Orfeón Donostiarra, Wiener Sängerknaben, and Coro Gulbenkian, among many others.

In 1997, the Palau de la Música Catalana was inscribed as part of Spain's tenth set of UNESCO World Heritage sites. It joined other iconic works of Antoni Gaudí, such as Casa Batlló, Casa Milà, Casa Vicens, Crypt of Colònia Güell, Nativity Façade and Crypt of the Basilica of the Sagrada Familia, Palau Güell, and Park Güell.

- Getting There

To reach the Palau de la Música Catalana, venture into the heart of Barcelona's historic center, just a stone's throw away from other cultural attractions like the Barcelona Cathedral, MUHBA - Museu d'Història de Barcelona, Plaça de Catalunya, and the famous Passeig de Gràcia, where you can find Gaudí's architectural wonders, Casa Batlló and Casa Milà.

Transportation options abound, including the metro lines 1 and 4 (Urquinaona station), RENFE and FGC trains (Plaça Catalunya station), and buses V15, V17, or 47 (Metro Urquinaona stop).

The Palau de la Música Catalana welcomes visitors daily from 9 am to 3 pm for guided tours in Catalan, Spanish, English, French, or Italian. Self-guided tours with an audio guide in multiple languages are available until 3:30 pm. Both tours last approximately 50 minutes.

- Tickets

Tickets can be purchased at the physical box office on Carrer de Sant Pere Més Alt or Carrer del Palau de la Música. However, I recommend booking them in advance through the official website to avoid any inconvenience. Ticket prices for self-guided tours are €15, while guided tours cost €19. Holders of the Barcelona Card can enjoy a direct 25% discount at the Palau de la Música Catalana.

Now, let's explore the stunning features of the Palau de la Música Catalana. As you enter, you'll be captivated by the Vestibule and its monumental double staircase, adorned with impressive lamps and columns made of marble and yellow glass. The Sala Lluís Millet, a waiting hall dedicated to the co-founder of the Orfeó Català, showcases vibrant stained glass windows and a magnificent modernist-style iron chandelier. The Terrace, accessible from Lluís Millet Hall, boasts a double colonnade covered in mesmerizing mosaics, offering a taste of the Palau's unique identity even before stepping inside.

The Concert Hall, the heart of the Palau de la Música, can accommodate over 2000 people. It is Europe's only auditorium lit entirely by natural light during the day, thanks to the stunning central skylight created by Antoni Rigalt i Blanch. The side walls feature stained glass windows, mosaic arches, and tile medallions honoring notable composers, while the ceiling is adorned with white and red ceramic roses and naturalistic motifs like flowers and peacock feathers.

The Stage, with its intricate sculptures and mosaics, pays homage to the choral society's heritage. Notably, the stage incorporates a female choir represented in the dome and features eighteen muses, half of which are sculptures and the other half mosaics. The Foyer, also known as Café Palau, offers a delightful dining experience with a restaurant, cafe, and bar, serving a range of meals and drinks throughout the day.

Camp Nou

For sports enthusiasts, a trip to Barcelona wouldn't be complete without stopping by the famed Camp Nou stadium, which is home to FC Barcelona's illustrious soccer club. Take a tour of the stadium to experience the history and ambiance of this renowned location.

Camp Nou, also known as the Nou Camp, is the iconic home stadium of FC Barcelona in La Liga. With a massive seating capacity of 99,354, it holds the title for the largest stadium in Spain, Europe, and the third-largest in the world. Currently, it is branded as Spotify Camp Nou due to sponsorship.

Construction of Camp Nou began in 1954 because Barcelona's previous stadium, Camp de Les Corts, had no space for expansion. Originally planned to be called Estadi del FC

46

Barcelona, it was eventually named Camp Nou, meaning "new field," which quickly gained popularity. The signing of László Kubala, one of Barcelona's greatest players, in June 1950 played a significant role in the decision to build a larger stadium.

Camp Nou was inaugurated on September 24, 1957, with a friendly match between FC Barcelona and a team of Hungarian stars, resulting in a 4-2 victory for the home team. Over the years, the stadium has hosted the European Cup/UEFA Champions League final three times (in 1979, 1989, and 1992) and the FIFA Club World Cup final in 2009 and 2011.

The stadium also features a dedicated museum that showcases the rich history of FC Barcelona. Visitors have the opportunity to take a tour of the stadium, which includes exploring the pitch, dressing rooms, and press room.

Camp Nou is situated in the Les Corts district of Barcelona and is easily accessible by public transportation. The closest metro stations are Palau Reial and Les Corts.

- Practical Information

If you're planning to visit Camp Nou, here's some practical information for you: The stadium and museum are open every day from 10:00 am to 6:30 pm. The museum has extended hours until 7:30 pm. Ticket prices for the stadium tour are €25 for adults and €20 for children, while tickets for the museum cost €23 for adults and €19 for children. The stadium tour takes approximately 1 hour and 30 minutes, while the museum tour lasts about 1 hour.

For more detailed information and updates, you can visit the official website of Camp Nou: https://www.fcbarcelona.com/en/club/facilities/spotify-camp-nou.

Chapter Three

Hidden Gems and Local Favorites

El Born Center for Culture and Memory

El Born Center for Culture and Memory, or El Born CCM for short, is housed in a former market hall, but what makes it unique is that they discovered archaeological remains of Barcelona's old city underneath the building. These remains date back to the Succession War of 1714, which was a pretty big deal in the history of Catalunya.

What's really neat about the museum is how they've displayed the ancient ruins. They dug out a large area of the floor to uncover the remains, and there are walkways surrounding the entire area, so you can get a real sense of what Barcelona looked like in the 17th and 18th centuries.

After Catalunya lost the war against the Borbonic army in 1714, its political freedom was taken away. The victorious side forced the residents of the La Ribera neighborhood to demolish their own homes to make room for a massive military fortress, aiming to control the city. This fortress, known as the Citadel, pointed its cannons inward at Barcelona as a constant reminder of its purpose. Eventually, the Citadel was demolished and replaced by Parc de la Ciutadella, meaning 'citadel' in reference to the fortress. The excavation at El Born CCM holds significant historical value as it reveals the remains of the demolished homes of La Ribera, offering insight into the aftermath of the War of Succession.

During the reign of King Philip V, who governed Catalunya with cruelty, the Catalan language was banned, and the region's autonomy was greatly reduced. Over a century later, in 1876, the El Born market was constructed. Designed by architect Josep Fontserè i Mestre and engineer Josep M. Cornet, the market was known for its unique iron architecture, a popular style among modernist architects at the time.

As Barcelona grew rapidly, the market became too small and closed in 1971. Initially, there were plans to demolish the building, but local protests led to its preservation. The idea then emerged to transform it into a library. However, during construction, significant 18th-century archaeological remains were discovered beneath the building, leading to a shift in plans. The locals, concerned about the neighborhood becoming overly touristy, voiced their opposition.

Archaeological research began in 1994, and in 2003, the decision was made to convert the building into a cultural center. It officially opened on September 11th, an important date for Catalunya. Initially called El Born CC (Cultural Center), the center now carries the additional letter 'M,' symbolizing 'memory' in Catalan.

Understanding the historical context and transformation of El Born CCM adds depth to your visit and appreciation of its significance as a cultural center.

If you're planning your visit, you can combine it with a stroll around the El Born neighborhood, a visit to the Picasso Museum, and maybe even have a picnic in the nearby Parc de la Ciutadella.

If you only want to see the free part of the museum, it'll take about 30 minutes. But if you want to check out the exhibition spaces, plan for about an hour or a bit more if you want to watch the video presentation on the history of Barcelona.

- Tips

You can reach the **Basilica of Santa Maria del Mar** via the Passeig del Born, a nice street with lots of bars and restaurants where you can stop for a tapa and a drink. Just remember that between 1pm and 5pm, you need to buy a ticket to enter.

El Born is also a great shopping area with interesting boutiques owned by local designers, so it's worth exploring if you're in the mood for some retail therapy.

If you brought the kids along, there's the **Parc de La Ciutadella** right behind El Born CCM. It's a wonderful spot for a picnic, and the children can play. Otherwise, you can even rent row boats.

If you want to take a closer look at the excavations, you'll need to book a guided tour. Make sure to check the agenda of El Born CCM as well, because they organize various activities like theater, workshops, exhibitions, and concerts.

- Tickets

Now, here's the best part: the entrance to El Born CCM is free! You can enter, walk around, and read the informational panels in English at your own pace. However, I recommend considering buying a ticket for a guided tour. The guide will take you down into the actual ruins and share interesting facts about ancient Barcelona. It's a really cool off the beaten path activity.

If you want to visit the permanent and temporary exhibits, there's a small fee, except on Sunday afternoons and the first Sunday of the month when it's free. The prices are reasonable, ranging from €3.08 for young people and seniors to €4.40 for adults.

- Opening Hours

The museum is closed on Mondays, except for holidays, but the other days of the week aren't usually crowded, so you can visit at any time that suits you.

El Born CCM is open from Tuesday to Sunday, from 10am to 8pm. Just keep in mind that it's closed on certain dates like New Year's Day, Labor Day, and Christmas.

If you want to visit for free, mark your calendar for Sunday afternoons from 3pm to 8pm or on specific holidays like Santa Eulàlia Day or La Mercè.

- Getting There

To get to El Born CCM, you can take the metro to Arc de Triomf on the red line (L1) and enjoy a pleasant 10-minute walk through Parc de la Ciutadella. If you prefer driving, there are parking garages around the area. You can also use the hop on-hop-off bus or cycle there if you're feeling adventurous.

Alternatively, you can walk from Plaça Catalunya in under half an hour, passing through interesting neighborhoods and even stopping by the Santa Maria del Mar basilica along the way.

- Highlights Of El Born CCM

As soon as you step inside, you'll be greeted by the fascinating excavations from the 18th century that were discovered here. They're below ground level and surrounded by a walkway, so you can walk around and explore them. There are informative boards in English that explain what you're seeing. If you want a closer look, you'll need to join a guided tour at specific times. El Born CCM is located in a stunning 19th-century market hall that underwent complete renovation in the 90s. It's a perfect blend of old architecture and modern design. Even if you only have a few minutes, it's worth walking in and taking a look around.

Inside the center, you'll find four distinct rooms with a mix of permanent and temporary exhibitions, a concert hall, a restaurant, and a museum shop.

- The Sala Villarroel

The Sala Villarroel is where you'll find the permanent exhibition called "Barcelona 1700, from stones to people." It showcases a vast collection of objects found during the excavation, ranging from everyday items like tableware and tobacco pipes to unique jewelry. You can get a glimpse into the daily life of 17th and 18th century Barcelona, see portraits of famous figures from that time, and explore the city's changing landscape through historical maps. There's also an informative movie in English that delves into the history of Barcelona.

- Sala Casanova

Sala Casanova is another room that hosts temporary exhibits, so make sure to check El Born CCM's website for the latest offerings.

- Sala Moragues

In Sala Moragues, you'll discover a concert hall with 280 seats and a beautiful grand piano on the stage. El Born CCM features a diverse program of concerts and performances, so it's worth checking their website for upcoming events.

- Sala Castellvi

If you're feeling hungry, head to Sala Castellvi, where you'll find the restaurant El 300 del Born, associated with the popular beer brand Moritz. Just note that after 8pm, access to the restaurant is from the street.

El Poble Sec neighborhood

A quaint area with several taverns, eateries, and cafes. It's the ideal location for a calm evening with friends.

Poble Sec is a neighborhood located in the Sants-Montjuïc district. The name Poble Sec means "dry village" in Catalan, and it is believed to be because the neighborhood lacked water sources for a long time. However, there is another theory that suggests the name came from factories drying up the water wells in the mid-nineteenth century. Poble Sec is situated between Montjuïc and Avinguda del Paral·lel and can be easily reached by Poble Sec (L3) and Paral·lel (L3) metro stations. It is surrounded by El Raval, Sant Antoni, and Sants-Montjuïc neighborhoods.

During the Middle Ages, the land outside Barcelona's city walls was used for agriculture, including orchards between the walls and Montjuïc. In the late 18th and early 19th centuries, manufacturing activities began to emerge in what is now Poble Sec. The medieval walls were demolished in 1854, and houses were built for workers from 1858 onwards. The neighborhoods of França Xica, Santa Madrona, and Huertas de San Beltrán were established and eventually grouped together under the name El Poble Sec.

Poble Sec Neighborhood Bucket List:

- Visit Refugi 307:

This is one of the bomb shelters built in Barcelona during the Spanish Civil War. It is one of the largest shelters and has tunnels spanning about 400 meters. It was well-equipped with various rooms for different purposes.

- See El Molino Theatre:

El Molino is a historic theatre dating back to 1898. It is known for its performances of music, theater, flamenco, burlesque, and cabaret.

- See Teatre Victoria:

The Victoria Theater opened in 1905 and has showcased musical productions like Monty Python's Spamalot and Grease.

- Visit Quimet & Quimet:

This family-run bar, established in 1914, offers superb tapas and montaditos (small open-faced sandwiches). It is located off the usual tourist track and is highly regarded.

- Visit Bodega 1900:

Bodega 1900, created by Albert Adrià, celebrates the local tradition of Sunday vermouth. It is part of the culinary projects by Albert Adrià in Poble Sec and Sant Antoni neighborhoods.

- Try Pakta:

Pakta, founded in 2013 by the Adrià brothers (Albert and Ferran) along with the Iglesias brothers, is a Michelin-starred restaurant offering Nikkei cuisine, a fusion of Peruvian and Japanese culinary traditions.

- Experience the Nightlife:

Sala Apolo: Known as one of the oldest dance halls in Europe, Sala Apolo has a rich history dating back to the early 20th century. It has transformed over the years, starting as an amusement park and evolving into a dance hall, bingo venue, professional skating club, and eventually a nightclub. In 2018, Sala Apolo celebrated its 75th anniversary with a documentary premiere. Since the 1990s, it has served as a concert hall and club, hosting numerous groups and DJs.

Mercat de Sant Antoni

This lively market sells meats, cheeses, fresh fruit, and seafood. It's a terrific spot to sample some regional cuisine.

The Mercat de Sant Antoni has a fascinating history that dates back to the mid-1800s when Barcelona's walls were demolished and the city underwent expansion. The market was designed by Antoni Rovira i Trias and occupies an entire block in the newly planned Eixample district. It was inaugurated in 1882 and was the first market to be located outside the medieval city perimeter.

While the Boqueria Market is often the first to come to mind when thinking of Barcelona markets, it is more of a tourist attraction. To experience the true local atmosphere, one should visit the Sant Antoni district. Located in the Eixample district, it is often overlooked by tourists due to the absence of Gaudi sites. However, it is highly popular among locals, particularly young hipsters, who are drawn to its trendy restaurants and vermouth tapas bars. So, if you want to see the real Barcelona and engage with the locals, Sant Antoni is the place to go.

The Mercat de Sant Antoni has a fascinating history that dates back to the mid-1800s when Barcelona's walls were demolished and the city underwent expansion. The market was designed by Antoni Rovira i Trias and occupies an entire block in the newly planned Eixample district. It was inaugurated in 1882 and was the first market to be located outside the medieval city perimeter.

While the Boqueria Market is often the first to come to mind when thinking of Barcelona markets, it is more of a tourist attraction. To experience the true local atmosphere, one should visit the Sant Antoni district. Located in the Eixample district, it is often overlooked by tourists due to the absence of Gaudi sites. However, it is highly popular among locals, particularly young hipsters, who are drawn to its trendy restaurants and vermouth tapas bars. So, if you want to see the real Barcelona and engage with the locals, Sant Antoni is the place to go.

Sant Antoni Bucket List

Explore the Medieval Ruins: The location of the Sant Antoni Market was once outside the gates of Barcelona's medieval walls. During the refurbishment of the marketplace in 2007, medieval and Roman ruins were discovered. While the Roman ruins are not yet open to the public, you can now see the medieval ruins in the basement of the market. These include part of the bastion and a sewerage system. Keep an eye out for updates from the Museum of History of Barcelona archaeologists working on the Roman ruins.

Visit the Food Stalls: Food has been sold at the Sant Antoni Market since its inception. After the recent renovation, the stalls have transformed into small food boutiques. Whether you enjoy cooking or simply appreciate quality food, visiting the food stalls is a must. One legendary stall to check out is Masclans, which has been selling salted cod since 1882. They offer delicious cod fritters and tuna pie, and you can even enjoy your snack at their small counter.

Additional Information

The food section of the Mercat de Sant Antoni is open from Monday to Saturday, from 8 AM to 8 PM. However, please note that on Mondays, many stalls are closed because there is no fresh fish available due to fishermen not going out fishing on Sundays. Additionally, after lunchtime, around 3 or 4 PM, many stalls may close as their produce sells out.

The clothes and accessories section of the market is open every day except Tuesday and Sunday, from 10 AM to 8:30 PM.

If you're interested in the flea market, it takes place every Sunday from 8:30 AM to 2 PM. This is a great opportunity to explore and find unique items.

Keep in mind that these opening hours may be subject to change, so it's always a good idea to double-check before your visit.

Carrer de Blai

You can have delectable small bites and a drink of wine at one of the pinchos bars here.

Carrer de Blai is renowned as the ultimate street for tapas in Barcelona. This vibrant city is known for its unique regional tapas like pà amb tomàquet and coca, which are beloved by both locals and visitors. While many touristic areas charge around 2€ or more for each tapa or pintxo, Carrer de Blai offers a different experience.

Bucket List of Must Visit Places on Carrer de Blai

- La Esquinita de Blai:

Located in the lively neighborhood of Poble Sec, right across from La Tasqueta de Blai, this spot goes beyond just pintxos. While they offer an impressive selection of affordable pintxos, La Esquinita de Blai also serves a variety of tapas and drinks. You can enjoy traditional favorites like patatas bravas, a sausage platter, seafood delights, and even their inventive Esquinita Hamburger with semi-cured manchego cheese. They are open from 9 a.m. to 1:30 a.m.

- Blai 9:

Prepare to feast your eyes on pintxos that are like works of art at Blai 9. It's advisable to arrive early, especially during the summer months, to secure a spot. Blai 9 welcomes guests from Monday to Sunday, from 12 pm to 12 am. You can find them at the intersection of Carrer de Salvà.

- Blai Tonight:

Also known as the Fábrica de Pinchos, this tapas bar and restaurant is famous for its amazing croquetas and a delightful variety of pintxos to satisfy your taste buds. It's an ideal spot for families and larger groups. Make sure to arrive early to secure a seat, preferably on their terrace. Blai Tonight operates from 6 p.m. to 1 a.m. and is located between Carrer del Poeta Cabanyes and Carrer de Tapioles.

- Pincho J:

This place is quite popular among the locals. They offer a diverse variety of tapas ranging from croquettes and seafood to meat and tortillas. Pincho J is a medium-sized restaurant, so finding a place to sit should be relatively easy. They operate from 12 pm to 12 am and can be found at the intersection of Carrer de Tapioles.

- La Tasqueta de Blai:

If you're craving tapas and pintxos with a meaty twist, this is the place to be. Their menu features sausages, mini hamburgers, and more. At La Tasqueta de Blai, you can enjoy the Andalusian deal, which includes a tapa with your Caña for less than 10£. The venue can accommodate around 25-30 people and remains open from 12:30 pm till 2 am. Look for them between Carrer de Salvà and Carrer del Poeta Cabanyes. As you stroll along Carrer Blai in the Poble-Sec neighborhood, you'll come across numerous other tapa and pintxo restaurants. Feel free to hop from one place to another until you find the perfect spot that suits your appetite.

- Getting There

All these restaurants and bars are nestled in the heart of the Sants-Montjuïc district, easily accessible via the Paral·lel metro stop, which can be reached by taking either line 2 (purple) or line 3 (green).

Recinto Modernista de Sant Pau

The Recinto Modernista de Sant Pau in Barcelona, Spain, is a true architectural masterpiece that pays homage to the Modernisme movement. Designed by the renowned architect Lluís Domènech i Montaner, this extraordinary complex was originally built as a hospital and symbolized innovation and healing. Its breathtaking architecture, featuring intricate details and vibrant mosaics, beautifully captures the essence of Catalan modernist style. Today, it holds the prestigious title of a UNESCO World Heritage site and has been transformed into a vibrant cultural center, inviting visitors to delve into its fascinating history, admire its remarkable architecture, and wander through its enchanting gardens.

The Recinto Modernista de Sant Pau is an exceptional example of the Art Nouveau style that flourished in the early 20th century, and its significance cannot be overstated. This expansive complex, initially designed for healthcare purposes, was a remarkable feat of modern engineering. With its innovative features like an underground tunnel system and well-planned courtyards, the campus facilitated the efficient movement of patients between buildings. Serving as a hospital until 2009, it now holds the esteemed distinction of being a UNESCO World Heritage Site.

One of the most captivating aspects of the Recinto Modernista de Sant Pau's history is its connection to the broader modernist movement that swept across Europe during the turn of the century. The intricate ceramic mosaics and stained glass windows adorning the buildings incorporate nature-inspired motifs and reflect the popular Art Nouveau style of the era. The architecture also draws heavily from Catalan Modernism, a movement that emerged in Barcelona during the late 19th century.

The design of the Recinto Modernista de Sant Pau showcases a harmonious blend of natural light and organic forms. Elaborate and colorful mosaics embellish the buildings, while intricate woodwork and stained glass windows adorn the interiors. The site's overall layout creates a perfect balance between the natural and the man-made, making it a captivating destination for architecture and design enthusiasts.

- Fun Facts about the Recinto Modernista de Sant Pau:

Symbolic Architecture: The architectural features of the Recinto Modernista de Sant Pau contain a wealth of hidden symbolism. By examining the sculptures and carvings closely, one can uncover intricate details that represent various aspects of Catalan culture and history.

Breathtaking Stained Glass: While the mosaics often steal the limelight, the complex also possesses magnificent stained glass windows embellishing some of the structures. These vibrant windows enhance the interior spaces with an additional touch of beauty.

Emphasis on Natural Light: The designers of the Recinto Modernista de Sant Pau prioritized natural lighting in their plans. They strategically positioned windows, skylights, and glass elements to maximize the penetration of sunlight into the interior, resulting in a bright and airy ambiance.

Healing Gardens: The gardens surrounding the complex are not only visually captivating but also serve as a home to a collection of ancient medicinal plants. Exploring these gardens at a leisurely pace allows one to discover the diverse flora and appreciate its historical significance.

Elaborate Ceramic Tiles: By observing the ceramic tiles adorning the buildings, one can encounter an array of intricate patterns and designs. These tiles were meticulously crafted and hand-painted, adding an artistic touch to the walls and floors.

Center of Medical Advancement: The Recinto Modernista de Sant Pau was not merely a hospital but also a center of medical innovation. It played a pioneering role in introducing groundbreaking advancements like X-ray technology during its time, contributing to the progress of medical science.

The Synchronization Clock: Located at the entrance of the Sant Salvador Pavilion, a unique clock known as the "Synchronization Clock" can be found. This clock served the purpose of synchronizing all the clocks within the complex, ensuring precise timekeeping throughout the hospital.

UNESCO Designated: In 1997, the Recinto Modernista de Sant Pau was recognized as a UNESCO World Heritage Site, acknowledging its cultural and historical significance.

Opened in: The complex opened its doors in 1905, serving as a hospital and contributing to the medical community.

Recinto Modernista Bucket List

Modernist Architecture: The Recinto Modernista de Sant Pau represents the epitome of modernist architecture. Marvel at its colorful stained glass, intricate mosaics, and ornate domes, making it one of Europe's most significant examples of Art Nouveau.

The Gardens: Enjoy the beauty of the lush gardens, perfect for a relaxing walk and capturing scenic photos. Explore different garden areas featuring a variety of plant species from around the world.

The Hospital Sant Pau Archive Room: Delve into the history of medical research spanning over a thousand years in the archive room. Discover fascinating information about medicine and the hospital itself.

The Dome Hall: During your guided tour, don't miss the Dome Hall. This light and airy space, adorned with stained glass, showcases exquisite architecture.

The Mosaic Hall: Be amazed by the vibrant tiles and stunning architecture in the Mosaic Hall, appreciating the incredible detail of the decorative mosaics.

The Pau's Pavilion: Explore the Pau's Pavilion, designed to accommodate children in need of care. Admire its bright and colorful mosaics and decorative elements.

- Opening Hours:

April to October: Open from 10 AM to 6:30 PM

November to March: Open from 10 AM to 5 PM

Visitors can enter until 30 minutes before closing time.

Closed on September 22nd and December 25th.

- Getting There:

By Bus: Convenient bus options include H8, 19, 47, 117, or 192. Get off at the Sant Antoni Maria Claret-Recinte Modernista stop, and it's just a short walk to the entrance.

By Metro: Take the L5 metro line and disembark at the Sant Pau - Dos de Maig station. From there, it's only a 5-minute walk to the entrance.

By Tram: If taking the tram, board the T4 tram to the Sant Pau stop. The entrance is just a 2-minute walk away.

By Car: Car parking is available at the Recinto Modernista de Sant Pau.

- Handy Information:

Suggested Duration: Plan for a 1-2 hour visit to fully appreciate the site.

Ticket Prices: Tickets start at €16.

The Montjuic Magic Fountain

This fountain performance is a breathtaking display of light, water, and music that you won't soon forget.

The Magic Fountain of Montjuïc, situated at the base of Montjuïc Mountain, has become a must-visit attraction in Barcelona. Its captivating display of music, light, and color draws both locals and tourists who gather around to witness the mesmerizing water choreography.

This enchanting fountain, located between the Palau Nacional and Avinguda de la Reina Maria Cristina, was originally built for the 1929 Universal Exposition by engineer Carles Buïgas. It wasn't until the 1980s that music was incorporated, and for the Barcelona '92 Olympic Games, the fountain underwent a complete restoration. In recent years, the fountain has embraced sustainability by replacing its traditional lighting with energy-efficient LED technology and utilizing phreatic water.

Since its inauguration, the Magic Fountain of Montjuïc has become an iconic symbol of Barcelona, illuminating the city with its dazzling lights and dancing water jets during important events. The fountain's lighting and hydraulic elements offer an astounding seven billion combinations of water and light. Throughout the day, at various times, around 2,600 liters of water per second dance to the rhythm of different types of music, including Disney melodies, classical compositions, soundtracks, and hits from the '80s and '90s. The fountain's signature song, however, is "Barcelona," the anthem of Barcelona '92, famously performed by Freddie Mercury and Montserrat Caballé at the fountain.

If you visit the Magic Fountain during the daytime, you'll encounter a magnificent fountain. It's a great opportunity to explore the Sants-Montjuïc area, which stretches from Montjuïc Mountain to the coastline. Some nearby attractions worth visiting include Montjuïc Mountain itself, the National Museum of Art of Catalonia, and Poble Espanyol.

At dusk,, I highly recommend visiting the Magic Fountain to witness the scheduled fountain show of light, water, and music. As the music begins, the fountain bursts into a dazzling array of colors and shades, with the water gracefully dancing to the rhythm of the melodies. This is the perfect time to enjoy the show, capture videos, and take photos as lasting mementos.

- Operating Hours

The operating hours of the Fountain of Montjuïc may vary depending on the time of year, but entry to the fountain show is free. The shows typically last between 10 and 15 minutes. For detailed information about the fountain's hours, how to get there, and more insights into its history, operation, and environmental sustainability, you can visit the official website of the Barcelona City Council.

Every year, the Magic Fountain is chosen as the venue for Piromusical, the grand finale of Barcelona's biggest festival.

Since it's a popular tourist attraction, it's advisable to arrive on time to secure the best spot to enjoy the show.

Treat yourself and your loved ones to a special night under the open sky at this captivating fountain.

Finding the best view to watch the Magic Fountain show can be a subjective experience, as there are no bad spots to enjoy the spectacle. However, if you're looking for a recommendation, we suggest positioning yourself at the top where the Museu Nacional d'Art de Catalunya (MNAC) is located. From this vantage point, you'll have a panoramic view of the entire fountain, allowing you to fully appreciate the vibrant colors and synchronized music.

Since the Magic Fountain is a popular attraction, it's a good idea to arrive early to secure your preferred spot. Keep in mind that on windy days, being too close to the fountain may result in some water spray due to the breeze. Therefore, finding a comfortable distance might be advisable.

Ultimately, the most important thing is to find a location that suits your preference and allows you to immerse yourself in the magical ambiance of the show. Enjoy the experience!

Schedule

To fully enjoy the Magic Fountain experience, it's important to be aware of its schedule as it doesn't operate every night and the timings vary throughout the year.

- Opening Hours

Here's a breakdown of the opening hours for different periods:

From November 1st to January 5th, the fountain is open on Thursdays, Fridays, and Saturdays from 8:00 PM to 9:00 PM, except for December 28th.

From January 7th to March 4th, the fountain is CLOSED for maintenance.

From March 5th to March 31st, it's open on Thursdays, Fridays, and Saturdays from 8:00 PM to 9:00 PM, except for March 27th and 28th.

From April 1st to May 31st, it's open on Thursdays, Fridays, and Saturdays from 8:00 PM to 10:00 PM.

From June 1st to September 30th, it's open on Wednesdays and Saturdays from 9:00 PM to 10:00 PM.

From October 1st to October 31st, it's open on Thursdays, Fridays, and Saturdays from 9:00 PM to 10:00 PM.

Please note that these schedules can be quite complex, so it's advisable to double-check the timetable to ensure the fountain is open on the day you plan to visit. The best part is that both the entrance and the entire show are free for everyone. So, make sure to enjoy this mesmerizing spectacle without any additional cost.

Montjuïc Mountain Bucket List

- MNAC Museum

When you're near the Magic Fountain, there are a few must-visit attractions worth exploring. One of them is the MNAC museum, boasting the largest collection of modern art in Catalonia. It's a fantastic opportunity to immerse yourself in the world of contemporary artistic expression.

- Visit the Castle

For breathtaking panoramic views of the city and its harbor, I recommend making the effort to climb to the top of Montjuic mountain and visit the Castle. From there, you'll be able to capture stunning photographs and take in one of the best vistas Barcelona has to offer.

- Poble Espanyol

Another nearby attraction is Poble Espanyol, originally constructed for the 1929 Universal Exposition. This unique destination showcases various architectural styles from different regions of Spain, providing a comprehensive representation of the country's rich cultural heritage.

Make sure to allocate some time during your visit to explore these attractions and enrich your experience near the Magic Fountain.

Location: Plaça de Carles Buïgas, 1, 08038 Barcelona

Bunkers del Carmel

A secret lookout point with expansive views of the city and the sea. It's also a fantastic location to see the sunset.

The Bunkers Barcelona is a true hidden gem and, without a doubt, one of our favorite spots in this incredible city. You might also hear it referred to as the Bunkers del Carmel, El Turó de la Rovira, or simply The Bunker. Nestled on a hilltop, this peaceful sanctuary offers some of the most breathtaking aerial views of BCN you can imagine.

Prepare to be mesmerized as you look out over the sea of terracotta rooftops that seem to stretch endlessly in every direction. From this vantage point, you'll be able to spot many of Barcelona's iconic landmarks, including the magnificent Sagrada Familia, the grand Palace of Montjuic, and the majestic surrounding mountains. And let's not forget the sweeping views of the picturesque coastline.

If you're seeking a unique and cost-free experience in Barcelona, visiting the bunkers is an absolute must. Immerse yourself in the rich history of El Turó de la Rovira, a hill of significant importance to the area. Its strategic 360-degree perspective has made it a site of constant occupation for centuries. During the tumultuous civil war from 1936 to 1939, it served as a defense against aerial attacks, housing anti-aircraft weaponry.

Though the guns are long gone, the weathered concrete defenses stand as a reminder of the past. Interestingly, the shelters were repurposed as slum housing, and a whole shanty town emerged in the surrounding area, housing 7% of Barcelona's population at one point. It wasn't until the 1990s, with the arrival of the Olympics and efforts to upgrade the city, that the shanty town was disbanded and its residents relocated.

For years, the Bunkers del Carmel remained forgotten, until the early 2000s when its unrivaled views started to attract attention once again. Now, visitors flock to this remarkable site to soak in its history and marvel at the panoramic vistas. You'll even find a small museum nestled within one of the bunkers, offering insights into the area's captivating past.

- Getting There

To reach the top of the Bunkers Barcelona, there are several options available, but be prepared for an uphill climb as it sits atop a 260-meter-tall mound. The ascent can take around half an hour, depending on the route you choose, your walking pace, and how often you stop to admire the unfolding views.

- By Metro

If you're taking the metro, there are two stations you can approach from: Guinardo / Hospital de Sant Pau or Alfons X. Both stations are on the Yellow Line 4, but Alfons X is slightly closer to the bottom of El Turó de la Rovira, where the path to the bunkers begins. It's advisable to get as close to the starting point as possible.

Once you arrive at Alfons X station, take the Ronda del Guinardo exit. Cross the road that leads down into an underground tunnel and turn left onto Carrer de Pere Costa. Then, take the first left onto Carrer de Thous. Follow this road until you reach a funky roundabout with a mini water fountain. Cross the roundabout directly, and you'll find yourself on Carrer de Tenerife, which leads to the bottom of the steps up to the Bunkers. This is where the steep climb begins. You'll know you're at the start when you spot a large playground on your right, complete with a dirt football pitch, ping pong tables, and a kids play area.

The stairs have a map and a sign that says "Escales de Tenerife," so it's virtually impossible to get lost from here. Even if the path splits at certain points, it always rejoins, so choose whichever route you prefer. As you ascend, towards the top of the stairs on your left, you'll see a large metal bridge that resembles a train track. Head towards it as you need to cross it. Once you're on the other side of the bridge, you'll see the bunkers above you, perched on the peak of the hill.

From this point, simply follow the paths that loop back on themselves until you reach the bunkers. Along the way, you might come across graffiti on the path that's directed towards tourists, expressing sentiments like "Tourist go home" or "Tourism kills this city." Don't let it discourage you. While there is a small anti-tourism movement in Barcelona, it certainly does not reflect the views of the majority.

- By Bus

If you prefer not to walk or find the 30-minute uphill climb challenging, taking the bus is a convenient option. There is a bus, the V17, that can take you closer to the top of El Turó de la Rovira than the metro stations.

To catch the V17 bus, find the nearest bus stop to your location. You can use a map to determine the closest stop. The V17 bus route starts from Port Vell and passes through the Gothic Quarter, Barceloneta, Urquinaona, Passeig de Gracia, and Gracia. If you're staying in one of these popular areas, there should be a stop nearby.

Stay on the bus until the final stop, Gran Vista - Pl de la Mitja Lluna. From there, it's quite clear how to get to the Bunkers. There is essentially only one route up, and it takes approximately 10 minutes.

It's worth noting that the bus approaches the Bunkers Barcelona from the El Carmel side of El Turó de la Rovira, which is the opposite side of the hill compared to the walking route.

- By Taxi

If you prefer not to use public transport or walk, another option to reach the top of El Turó de la Rovira is by taking a taxi. Keep in mind that this will be the most expensive method of transportation.

The taxi will drop you off at the same point as the bus stop, as it's not possible to drive any further. The cost of the taxi ride will depend on your starting point and the type of taxi you choose. Uber is available in Barcelona and may offer slightly lower fares compared to regular taxi cabs.

Once you're dropped off, you'll still need to walk for about 10 minutes to reach the Bunkers Barcelona. As mentioned before, simply follow the route that leads upward towards the top.

The Bunkers Barcelona offers a unique experience, and the best time to visit is during sunset. The soft, golden light enhances the city's beauty and creates a majestic atmosphere. However, keep in mind that sunset is a popular time, and it can get crowded. If you prefer a more serene experience, consider visiting at sunrise when you're likely to have the place to yourself.

At the Bunkers Barcelona, there aren't any specific activities or attractions other than enjoying the breathtaking views. It's a place to unwind and take in the panoramic vistas of the city. Unlike places like Tibidabo or Montjuic, there are no thrill rides or fountain shows. The Bunkers Barcelona offers a tranquil and laid-back atmosphere, perfect for soaking in the stunning aerial views of Barcelona.

El Raval

The stylish and cosmopolitan district is home to street art, antique stores, and excellent restaurants.

El Raval is a lively and diverse neighborhood located in the heart of Barcelona. It is renowned for its vibrant and bohemian atmosphere, housing some of the city's top museums and restaurants. El Raval is surrounded by other neighborhoods like Sant Antoni, the Gothic Quarter, and El Poble Sec.

The name "Raval" is derived from the Arabic word "rabad," which means outskirts. Initially, El Raval was situated outside the Roman walls of Barcino and the first set of medieval walls. However, it was later enclosed within the second set of medieval walls. You can still see remnants of the medieval walls near the Drassanes.

Interestingly, the layout of El Raval was influenced by old Roman roads outside Barcino. In the tenth century, the monastery of Sant Pau del Camp served as the area's first significant center. As Barcelona expanded, El Raval became enveloped within a third city wall.

During the Middle Ages, El Raval primarily consisted of market gardens that supplied the city with fresh produce. The industrialization of the neighborhood took place between 1770 and 1840. To accommodate workers from rural areas employed in textile mills, multi-story tenement blocks were constructed, maximizing limited space.

What to See and Do in El Raval

- Art in Public Spaces

One of the must-see sights in El Raval is Botero's Cat, a chubby bronze sculpture that has become an iconic symbol of the neighborhood. Located at the end of Rambla del Raval, it serves as a popular meeting point before a night out. Another notable artwork is the rounded horse created by renowned artist Fernando Botero, which can be found at Terminal 2 of Barcelona El Prat Airport.

El Gato De Botero

- Street Art

El Raval boasts a thriving street art scene, with famous street artists like Space Invader leaving their marks around the neighborhood. Keep an eye out for impressive graffiti and murals as you explore the streets of El Raval.

- Museums

The Museu Marítim de Barcelona, housed in the historic Drassanes (Royal Dockyards), offers a fascinating glimpse into Barcelona's maritime history. Construction of the dockyards began in the 13th century, and the museum showcases a replica of the Galera Reial (Royal Galley) along with other maritime artifacts.

- MACBA

For contemporary art enthusiasts, the Museu d'Art Contemporani de Barcelona (MACBA) is a must-visit. The museum features a permanent collection of over 5,000 works from the mid-20th century onwards. It is located in Plaça dels Àngels, a popular hangout spot for young people, where you can also witness skateboarders showcasing their skills.

- CCCB

Next to MACBA, you'll find the Centre de Cultura Contemporània de Barcelona (CCCB), a dynamic institution that hosts various exhibitions, debates, festivals, concerts, films, courses, and workshops, offering a diverse range of cultural experiences.

- Architecture and Palaces

Marvel at the Art Nouveau-inspired Palau Güell, designed by the renowned architect Antoni Gaudí for the Güell i López family. This magnificent palace, constructed between 1886 and 1888, showcases Gaudí's distinctive style. Note that the family later moved to Park Güell, another architectural masterpiece by Gaudí.

the La Virreina Centre de la Imatge

Within the baroque and rococo Palau de la Virreina, you'll find the La Virreina Centre de la Imatge. This museum houses works by prominent contemporary Catalan artists like Oriol

Bohigas and Antoni Abad. Entrance to the museum is free, allowing visitors to enjoy the rich artistic expressions of Catalonia.

If you're looking for an unforgettable night out, El Raval has a vibrant nightlife scene that caters to different tastes. Here are some notable venues to check out:

- Moog:

Since its establishment in 1996, Moog has been a go-to destination for underground techno and electronic music lovers. This intimate club has hosted performances by renowned international DJs, offering an immersive experience for electronic music enthusiasts.

- La Confiteria:

Step back in time at La Confiteria, a former confectionary store that dates back to 1912. This beautifully preserved establishment, located in the heart of the theater district, now serves as a cocktail bar and restaurant. Enjoy a unique atmosphere and indulge in delicious drinks while surrounded by historic charm.

- JazzSí Club:

If you appreciate live music, JazzSí Club is a must-visit. Associated with the Taller de Músics, a prestigious Catalan music school, this club hosts concerts and jam sessions featuring a variety of genres, including jazz, blues, flamenco, and Cuban music. Immerse yourself in the vibrant sounds of talented musicians and experience the lively atmosphere of this dynamic venue.

Please Note: Safety in El Raval

While El Raval has undergone significant gentrification and development in central Barcelona, it is important to be aware of the neighborhood's reputation for certain safety concerns. Carrer d'En Roig and similar streets have gained notoriety for the presence of illegal drug activities, such as narcopisos (flats illegally occupied by drug dealers). Additionally, like in many parts of the city, incidents of robberies and pickpocketing can occur.

To ensure your safety while exploring El Raval, it is essential to exercise caution and employ common sense, particularly when venturing out at night. Here are some tips to keep in mind:

Stay vigilant: Be aware of your surroundings and keep a close eye on your belongings, especially in crowded areas or tourist hotspots.

Use secure bags: Opt for bags that have sturdy closures and keep them close to your body to minimize the risk of theft.

Avoid displaying valuables: Keep expensive items, such as jewelry and electronics, concealed and avoid drawing unnecessary attention to yourself.

Stay on well-lit and populated streets: Stick to main streets with ample lighting and pedestrian activity, particularly during nighttime.

Stay informed: Stay updated on the current safety situation in El Raval by consulting local authorities, tourist information centers, or trusted sources.

Plaça Felip Neri

A tranquil square with a tragic past that is tucked away in the Gothic Quarter. It's a treasure.

Plaça de Sant Felip Neri, nestled near the Cathedral, is undeniably one of Barcelona's most enchanting and serene squares. While it exudes an air of romance, the history tied to this place is tragically poignant. The scars on the church walls are a somber reminder of the terrible events that unfolded here.

Fountain at Plaça Felip Neri

To understand the significance, we must delve into the era of Franco and the Spanish Civil War. Barcelona, serving as the Republican capital, became a defiant city that Franco sought to conquer.

With support from Hitler and Mussolini, Franco's Nationalist forces had already triumphed over numerous Republican fronts. However, Barcelona remained beyond his grasp. In January 1938, Franco initiated air raids on the city, causing extensive devastation throughout the year. The fateful day for Plaça Sant Felip Neri arrived on January 30, 1938. A bomb unleashed by Franco's forces struck the square, claiming the lives of 30 people, mostly children seeking refuge in the basement of the Church of Sant Felip Neri. As bystanders rushed to aid the victims, a second bomb struck, causing 12 more casualties. The square and surrounding buildings were left in ruins, and the church bore the scars of the tragedy. In the aftermath, the city decided to renovate the square, enlarging it and creating an access point, Carrer de Montjuïc del Bisbe, which had previously been sealed off.

The bombing remains the most well-known and haunting tale associated with the square. The memory of the Barcelona bombings still lingers vividly in the hearts and minds of the locals. A memorial plaque was installed on January 30, 2007, on the facade of the Sant Felip Neri convent beneath a circular window, serving as a poignant tribute to the victims.

Yet, the square's dark past stretches further back in history. Before Franco's assault, it was a medieval Jewish cemetery known as the Cementiri de Montjuïc del Bisbe. However, the arrival of the black plague and famine in the 14th century led to the demise of the Jewish community, unjustly blamed for the hardships. The Jewish Quarter, El Call, was attacked, eventually leading to its destruction in 1391.

Afterward, the square came under the ownership of the Cathedral of Barcelona, which used the land as its cemetery. Here, Cathedral parishioners, as well as members of brotherhoods and guilds with assigned altars in the cathedral, found their final resting place. The area became known as the Fossar dels Condemnats (Grave of the Condemned), where criminals deemed guilty were executed by hanging or stoning before being buried.

Location: You can find it at Plaça Sant Felip Neri, 5, 08002 Barcelona.

Getting there: Take the metro Line 3 (to Liceu) or Line 4 (to Jaume I). You can also reach it by bus using lines L14, 45, 59, 91, 120, and V15 (to Plaça Sant Jaume).

Cost: It's completely free of charge.

Chapter Four

Culture and Arts

Museums

Museu Picasso

Pablo Picasso's life and art are celebrated in the Museu Picasso, which houses more than 4,000 exhibitions.

The Picasso museum can be found right in the heart of Barcelona, in the trendy El Born district. This neighborhood is known for its cozy atmosphere, trendy vibe, and abundance of bars, cafes, and artsy shops. It's the perfect place to get lost and wander through its medieval narrow streets, immersing yourself in the vibrant energy of the city.

The museum is located on Carrer Montcada street, specifically at numbers 15-23. This street is steeped in history, featuring medieval palaces and often bustling with visitors.

Highlights and Must-Sees of Museu Picasso

The Picasso collection is housed in five Gothic palaces, each with its own unique history. The art pieces themselves are not the only special aspect here; the buildings themselves are remarkable. Together, they house one of the largest collections of Picasso's works in the world, making it a must-visit for art enthusiasts.

- Palace Aguilar

This palace, dating back to the 13th century, has undergone several alterations over the years until the 18th century. It was owned by Berenguer de Aguilar, who purchased it from the Coromines-Desplà bourgeois family around the year 1400. During a renovation, an impressive fresco from 1229 depicting the conquest of Majorca was discovered. The central courtyard features an open staircase and a gallery of pointed Gothic arches, showcasing typical medieval architectural elements.

- Palace Baró de Castellet

This palace is named after its owner, Mariano Alegre de Aparici i de Amat, who was granted the noble title of Baron de Castellet by King Carlos IV. The structure of this palace is similar to the others, with a central courtyard and an open staircase. On its facade, you'll find an interesting relief with a religious theme from the 16th century. Inside, the main floor boasts a neoclassical hall adorned with marble and polychrome elements from the mid-18th century.

- Palace Meca

Built between the 13th and 14th centuries, this palace was owned by Jaime Caballero, an advisor to the Barcelona City Council, in 1349. It later became the most important palace in the neighborhood under the ownership of Ramón Desplà y Caballero, Jaime's grandson. The palace went through various owners, but its name comes from José Meca y Cazador, an important marquis from the Cassador saga. Like the other palaces, it features a central courtyard and medieval coffered ceilings on the main floor, displaying vibrant polychrome decorations.

- Casa Mauri

Dating back to the 18th century, Casa Mauri is believed to have been built on top of much older structures, potentially from the Roman era. The facade of Casa Mauri showcases a unique and beautiful wooden lattice, which is a rarity in Barcelona. The building has had different owners throughout its history, even serving industrial purposes at one point. In 1999, it was acquired by the Picasso Museum, adding to its rich historical significance.

- Palace Finestres

This palace dates back to the 13th century and was constructed on top of a Roman necropolis. The original owners are unknown until it was acquired by the Dalmases family in

1698. In 1872, José Vidal y Torres, the owner of Casa Mauri, purchased the palace and connected it to his own house. Palace Finestres showcases intriguing details from the 13th century, including a coffered ceiling and two windows with columns, which are characteristic of the time period. Today, the palace is used as a temporary exhibition space.

- Tickets

Tickets for the Picasso Museum can be purchased at the entrance, but keep in mind that it can get very busy, especially during the summer. To avoid long lines and crowds, the best option is to buy your tickets online and make sure to arrive on time. Simply show the ticket on your smartphone at the entrance and you're good to go. Take a look at our facts and ticket options to choose what works best for you and get ready for a cozy and unique museum experience.

- Hours

Here are some important details to note:

Opening hours: Monday from 10:00 AM to 5:00 PM, Tuesday to Sunday from 9:00 AM to 7:00 PM, and Thursday from 9:00 AM to 9:30 PM.

Closed dates: The museum is closed on January 1st, May 1st, June 24th, and December 25th.

Special schedule on certain dates: On January 5th, the museum operates from 9:00 AM to 5:00 PM, and on December 24th and 31st, it operates from 9:00 AM to 2:00 PM.

Please note that ticket sales will end 30 minutes before the closing time, and sales may also end earlier if tickets are sold out.

- Getting There

By Metro: Take Line 4 and get off at Jaume I station. Alternatively, you can take Line 1 and get off at Arc de Triomf station.

By Bus: Various bus routes can take you to different stops near the museum. You can take buses 120, 45, V15, V17, and Via Laietana stop; buses 39, 51, and H14 at Passeig Picasso stop; or buses H14, 45, 51, and Princesa stop.

Palau Nacional

The stunning Palau Nacional houses the National Museum of Catalan Art, showcasing a wide range of artwork spanning from the Romanesque era to the mid-20th century.

90

Standing proudly on Montjuïc hill, the Palau Nacional was originally constructed for the 1929 International Exhibition. Today, it serves as the home of the National Art Museum of Catalonia.

The spacious esplanade surrounding the National Palace offers some of the most breathtaking views of the city. You'll find other notable attractions nearby, including the Mies van der Rohe Pavilion, the Magic Fountain, and the Fundació Joan Miró, where you can admire the works of the renowned Surrealist artist, Joan Miró.

During the 1929 Exhibition, the National Palace attracted significant attention, captivating the crowds that flocked to the Catalan region for the event. Although originally designed by Catalan architect Josep Puig i Cadafalch, the project was taken over by dictator Primo de Rivera, resulting in a more nationalist-style design created by architects Enric Català and Pedro Cendoya.

The result is a grand Neo-Baroque building featuring a central dome and several towers. The magnificent Oval Hall underwent renovation in 1992, just in time for the Summer Olympics held in Barcelona that year. The rest of the building was renovated in the early 21st century by architects Gae Aulenti and Josep Benedito.

The MNAC, also known as the Museu Nacional d'Art de Catalunya, is situated within the majestic Palau Nacional, a splendid Neo-Baroque palace. This iconic museum building is perched at the foot of Montjuïc, a picturesque mountain that graces the city of Barcelona.

The MNAC is a must-visit destination for art enthusiasts. As the largest museum in Catalonia, it boasts an extensive collection that spans various periods and styles.

The museum is renowned for its Romanesque Art collection, considered the most significant in the world. Visitors can admire captivating frescoes from the 12th and 13th centuries, many of which were originally housed in Pyrenean churches and later brought to the museum.

In addition to the Romanesque treasures, the Palau Nacional showcases an array of remarkable works from the Gothic, Renaissance, and Baroque periods. Esteemed artists such as Goya, El Greco, and Peter Paul Rubens are represented, allowing visitors to appreciate their masterpieces up close.

The MNAC also features stunning decorative art from the 19th and 20th centuries, including furniture and chandeliers. Many of these pieces embody the distinctive style of Barcelona's beloved Modernist movement, also known as Art Nouveau in other parts of the world. It's a feast for the eyes and a testament to the city's artistic heritage.

- How to Get There

The MNAC can be easily accessed by public transportation. The nearest metro station is Espanya, which is served by multiple lines including L1, L3, L8, S33, S4, S8, R5, and R6. If you prefer a hop-on-hop-off experience, you can take the Bus

Turístic that stops at the MNAC. Additionally, there is parking available nearby for those traveling by car.

- Opening Hours

During the winter season from 1st October to 30th April, the MNAC is open from Tuesdays to Saturdays between 10:00 AM and 6:00 PM. In the summer season from 1st May to 30th September, the museum extends its opening hours, operating from Tuesdays to Saturdays between 10:00 AM and 8:00 PM. On Sundays and holidays, the museum welcomes visitors from 10:00 AM to 3:00 PM. Please note that the MNAC is closed on Mondays, except on public holidays. It is also closed on 1st January, 1st May, and 25th December.

- Admission Fees

The normal admission fee for the MNAC is €12.00, which is valid for two consecutive days. Students can enjoy a 30% discount on the admission price. Children under 16 years of age and seniors aged 65 and above can enter the museum for free. There are also specific dates when admission is free, including the 1st Sunday of the month, 12th February, 18th May, and 11th + 24th September. Visitors with the Barcelona Card and the Articket Barcelona can also enjoy free admission to the MNAC.

Fundació Joan Miró

The Fundació Joan Miró, also known as the Joan Miró Foundation, is a museum dedicated to modern art that pays tribute to the renowned artist Joan Miró. It is situated on the picturesque hill of Montjuïc.

in Barcelona, you'll encounter the art of Joan Miró all around you. From the moment you arrive at the airport and see the impressive mosaic featuring Miró's work to spotting his iconic star in the logo of la Caixa bank, his art is an integral part of the city.

Joan Miró Museum

If you're interested in exploring more of Miró's art, I recommend visiting the Miró Museum, also known as the Fundació Joan Miró. You can enjoy free admission to the museum with the Articket and the Burcelona Card, which is a great way to save some money while immersing yourself in Miró's creations.

To reach the Miró Museum, you can conveniently take the Bus Turístic, which provides easy access to many popular attractions in the city.

While you're in the area, don't miss the opportunity to visit the Parc de Joan Miró, located near Plaça Espanya and behind the Las Arenas department store. Here, you'll find Miró's "Dona i Ocell" (Woman and Bird), a vibrant and symbolic tribute to the unity of man and woman.

If you happen to arrive in Barcelona by cruise ship and disembark at the harbor, you'll even be greeted by Miró's round mosaic face along the famous Ramblas.

Make sure to set aside some time to explore Miró's works at the Fundació Joan Miró. You can take a leisurely walk from Plaça Espanya, passing by the MNAC, the Catalonian national museum, and through the charming Jardí de les Escultures, which will lead you straight to the museum. It's a worthwhile experience for any art lover or enthusiast.

The Miró Museum, also known as the Fundació Joan Miró, was established by the artist himself and opened its doors on June 10, 1975. Joan Miró generously donated a majority of his works to the foundation, and additional pieces were contributed by his wife Pilar Juncosa, Joan Prats, and Kazumasa Katsutas. Among the notable works in the collection are the "Couple d'Amoureux aux Jeux de Fleur d'Amandier" (1975) and a large, intricately designed wall hanging created specifically for the foundation.

With over 10,000 paintings, drawings, sculptures, stage designs, and carpets, the museum boasts the largest collection of Joan Miró's works. The collection spans Miró's career, with the earliest drawings dating back to 1901. On the rooftop terrace, visitors can admire Miró's vibrant sculptures while enjoying a splendid view of Barcelona.

Miró's vision was to create an international, interdisciplinary center that would make art accessible to the public. The foundation continues to organize rotating contemporary exhibitions from the 20th and 21st centuries, along with academic research projects and cultural events. One highly recommended event is the "Nits de música" (nights of music), featuring classical music performances by international artists every Thursday. In recognition of its excellence, the center received the European Museum of the Year Award in 1977.

The Museum Building, designed by Josep Lluís Sert, showcases the close friendship and collaboration between Sert and Miró. Both shared a penchant for harmonious forms, playing with light, space, and colors. Their love for nature and Catalonia is evident in the distinct architectural feature of the inner courtyard, with rooms arranged in a centrifugal manner around it. This architectural element, known as the "Impluvium," is commonly found in Catalan monasteries and palaces dating back to Roman times.

During Franco's dictatorship, Sert served as the head of the School of Design at Harvard University in the United States, becoming the first internationally renowned Spanish architect.

In 1929, he founded GATPAC (Grup d'Arquitectes i Tècnics per al Progrés de l'Arquitectura Contemporània) to promote the modernization and development of Spanish architecture. Sert drew inspiration from renowned architects such as Wright, Gropius, Mies Van Der Rohe, and his mentor Le Corbusier, which is reflected in his rational and pragmatic style.

The museum building's clean and cubist shapes, rendered in white, give it a light and flowing appearance, while creating a sense of spaciousness within the rooms. The offset arrangement of the interior spaces, intertwined with bright patios and terraces, brings dynamism, transparency, and ample natural light to the building's interior. Sert prioritized flexibility and movement, ensuring spatial continuity while allowing visitors to experience the artwork from various perspectives.

The building underwent expansions in 1986 and 2000, and in 2002, it received the "Twenty-Five Year Award" from the American Institute of Architects. From the museum terrace, visitors can enjoy a stunning view of Barcelona's architectural landscape. After exploring the exhibitions, taking a break at the museum café surrounded by Miró's sculptures is a delightful option. Don't forget to visit the museum library, which houses the artist's personal book collection, providing further insight into Miró's artistic journey.

Address:

Avinguda Miramar, 71-75, Parc de Montjuïc

Phone: +34 934 439 470

Website: www.fmirobcn.org/en/

- Getting There:

Metro: Take the Paral·lel line (L2, L3) and then transfer to the Funicular de Montjuïc (cable car).

Bus Turístic: Stop at Fundació Joan Miró.

Parking available nearby.

- Opening Times:

Tuesday - Saturday: 10:00 AM - 8:00 PM

Sunday: 10:00 AM - 6:00 PM

Access to the Foundation is available until 30 minutes before closing.

Closed on Mondays, except on January 2nd, April 10th and 24th, May 1st, June 5th, September 11th and 25th, 2023.

- Admission:

Regular ticket: €14.00

Students, seniors (65+): €7.00

Children up to 14 years old: Free

Free admission with the Barcelona Card and the Articket Barcelona.

The Museu d'Història de Barcelona

A historical museum that showcases artifacts and exhibits from Roman times to the present.

The Museum of the History of Barcelona (MUHBA) is a captivating museum that showcases the rich history of the city, from its ancient Roman origins to the present day.

Located in the Gothic Quarter on Plaça del Rei, the museum's main headquarters are housed in a remarkable building called Padellàs House. This historic structure features a stunning Gothic courtyard and serves as the entrance to the museum.

One of the highlights of the museum is the extensive archaeological underground area beneath Plaça del Rei. Covering over 4.000 square meters, visitors can explore the remains of the ancient Roman city of Barcino. The underground exhibition provides insights into daily life in Roman houses, including various aspects such as factories (such as laundry, dyeing, salted fish and garum production, and wineries), shops, walls, and streets. Additionally, the remains of the early Christian and Visigothic Episcopal architectural complex, including a cross-shaped church, bishop's palace, and baptistery, can also be discovered.

Within the medieval Royal Palace, visitors can enjoy a small exhibition that outlines Barcelona's medieval history beneath the magnificent Romanesque vaults. The museum's collection also extends to other sites throughout the city, including archaeological sites, the Jewish quarter, industrial buildings, and sites associated with renowned architect Antoni Gaudí and the Spanish Civil War.

Address: Plaça del Rei / Carrer del Veguer 2, Barcelona

Metro: The nearest metro station is Jaume I.

- Tickets:

Adults: €7

Visitors aged 16-25 and 65+: €5

Children aged 0-16: Free entry

The museum offers free admission on Sundays after 3:00 pm.

- Opening hours:

Tuesday to Saturday: 10:00 am - 7:00 pm (On Wednesdays, it is open until 8:00 pm).

Sundays and public holidays: 10:00 am - 2:30 pm

Closed on Mondays, January 1 and 6, May 1, June 10, and December 25/26.

Museu d'Art Contemporani de Barcelona

The Museum of Contemporary Art of Barcelona, or MACBA for short, focuses on showcasing artworks created during the latter half of the 20th century. Renowned American architect Richard Meier was entrusted with the design of the museum.

Meier's design aims to harmoniously blend the contemporary artworks displayed inside with the architectural styles of the surrounding historic buildings.

Upon entering MACBA, visitors are greeted by a cylindrical hall that leads to various exhibition galleries through a series of mechanical ramps. The exhibition encompasses visual art in various mediums, including paintings, photographs, films, and installations.

Currently, the museum features works by artists such as Matta, Fahlstrom, Brassaï, Palazuelo, Roth, Broodthaers, Spero, Balcells, and Creischer. These artists contribute to the diverse and engaging collection on display at MACBA.

- Opening Hours:

Monday to Friday: 10:00 am — 8:00 pm

Tuesday (except public holidays): Closed

Saturday: 10:00 am — 8:00 pm

Sunday and public holidays: 10:00 am — 3:00 pm

Please note that the last entry and ticket purchases are available up to 30 minutes before closing time. The exhibition rooms will start closing 15 minutes before the official closing time. The museum is closed on 1 January and 25 December.

Opening hours may vary on certain public holidays:

6 January: 10:00 am — 3:00 pm

7 and 10 April: 10:00 am — 8:00 pm

1 May: 10:00 am — 3:00 pm

5 June: 10:00 am — 3:00 pm

24 June: 10:00 am — 8:00 pm

15 August: 10:00 am — 8:00 pm

11 and 25 September: 10:00 am — 8:00 pm

12 October: 10:00 am — 3:00 pm

1 November: 10:00 am — 3:00 pm

6, 8 and 26 December: 10:00 am — 3:00 pm

Please take note of these special opening hours on specific dates.

CosmoCaixa - Science Museum

Welcome to the interactive science museum, CosmoCaixa! This incredible museum, with its modernisme architecture, is not only one of the largest in Barcelona and Spain, but also one of the most exciting. It was built at a cost of 100 million euros and opened its doors in 2005.

As you enter the museum, you'll be greeted by none other than Albert Einstein himself. A lifelike statue of the renowned physicist stands near the information desk in the entrance hall, setting the tone for the exploration of scientific wonders that await.

Prepare to embark on a fascinating journey as you descend 30 meters down to the 5th basement floor. The descent takes you along a gigantic spiral path, wrapped around a tropical tree from the Amazon region called Acariquara. It's an awe-inspiring sight that adds to the unique experience of the museum.

CosmoCaixa is widely recognized as one of Europe's most prestigious museums, and it is operated by the social

Foundation "la Caixa." It offers an array of interactive exhibits and educational displays that will captivate visitors of all ages.

- Practical details:

Address:

Teodor Roviralta, 47-51

Website:

www.fundaciolacaixa.es

Getting There:

Metro: Take the Av. del Tibidabo (FGC, L7), then it's an 800-meter walk or a short bus ride.

Bus Turístic: Tramvia Blau - Tibidabo, then continue with Bus 196.

Parking is available nearby for your convenience.

- Opening Hours:

The museum is open from Tuesday to Sunday, from 10:00 am to 8:00 pm. Please note that it is closed on Mondays, except for public holidays. Additionally, the museum remains closed on 25 December, 1 January, and 6 January.

- Admission:

The regular admission fee is €4.00. However, children under 16 years old can enter for free. If you have the Barcelona Card, you can enjoy free admission to CosmoCaixa.

Museu del Disseny

The Museu del Disseny de Barcelona, also known as the Barcelona Design Museum, is a dynamic center that promotes the understanding and appreciation of the design world. It serves as both a museum and a laboratory, fostering creativity and innovation. The museum focuses on four main design disciplines: space design, product design, information design, and fashion.

This impressive institution is the result of the merger of several previously existing museums, including the Museu de les Arts Decoratives, the Museu Tèxtil i d'Indumentària, and the Gabinet de les Arts Gràfiques collection. By combining these resources, the Barcelona Design Museum offers a comprehensive exploration of design in its various forms.

In 2014, the museum unveiled its new headquarters, located on Plaça de les Glòries, near the iconic Torre Agbar. This modern and vibrant space provides a fitting setting for the exhibitions and activities that take place, engaging visitors in an immersive design experience.

104

Whether you have a passion for space design, product design, information design, or fashion, the Barcelona Design Museum offers a rich and diverse collection that will captivate your imagination. Step into a world where creativity meets functionality, and discover the power of design to shape our surroundings.

- Address:

Plaça de les Glòries, Barcelona

Website:

www.museudeldisseny.cat

Plan your visit to the Barcelona Design Museum and be inspired by the ingenuity and beauty of design in all its forms.

- Tickets

General price: 6 €

Reduced price: 4 €

For temporary exhibitions, it is recommended to check the prices on the museum's website. Tickets can be purchased at the museum reception.

There is a reduced price of 4.20 € available as well.

- Getting There

To get to the museum, you can take the Barcelona Bus Turístic or the Barcelona City Tour.

Free admission is offered on Sunday afternoons from 3 to 8 pm, as well as on the first Sunday of each month. Additionally, the museum has open days on February 12 (Saint Eulàlia's Day) and September 24 (La Mercè), where admission is also free.

Museu Frederic Marès

Sculptor Frederic Marès's private collection of artwork and artifacts, on display in the Museu Frederic Marès, spans antiquity, the Middle Ages, and the Renaissance.

The Museu Frederic Marès is a significant sculpture museum in Spain, showcasing the extensive collection of sculptor Frederic Marès. Throughout his lifetime from 1893 to 1991, Marès passionately gathered statues and various curiosities. The museum houses one of the most important collections of Spanish sculptures spanning from the 12th to the 19th century. It is situated in a former palace of the Inquisition in the Barri Gòtic district, just behind the cathedral.

The Museu is divided into two main sections: the Sculpture Collection and the Collector's Cabinet.

In the Sculpture Collection, you'll find a remarkable display of artworks from different regions of Spain, spanning a wide range of time periods from pre-Roman to the 19th century. This collection includes significant pieces from the Middle Ages, such as polychrome religious carvings, Romanesque capitals and reliefs, including those created by the renowned sculptor Master Cabestany. You'll also encounter Gothic altarpieces and the ornate coffins used for knights' burials. The museum also features examples of Spanish Renaissance and baroque sculptures, representing various schools of sculpture throughout history, from medieval times to the modern era.

The "Gabinet del Col·leccionista" (Collector's Cabinet) offers a fascinating glimpse into the daily lives of our ancestors from the 15th to the 19th centuries. This section showcases a collection of meticulously crafted objects that provide insights into the customs and traditions of the past. The Collector's Cabinet is divided into three galleries, each offering a unique perspective on the artifacts that offer a glimpse into the everyday lives of previous generations.

- Opening Hours

Tuesday to Saturday: 10am to 7pm

Sunday and public holidays: 11am to 8pm

Please note that the museum is closed on the following dates: January 1st, May 1st, June 24th, and December 25th. Make sure to plan your visit accordingly and check for any updates or changes to the opening hours before your visit.

Museu Egipci de Barcelona

Ancient Egyptian artifacts and displays on subjects including everyday life, religion, and mythology can be found here.

The Egyptian Museum of Barcelona boasts an impressive collection of Egyptian art and culture, making it a top destination for enthusiasts. Spanning over 2,000 square meters, the museum takes visitors on a captivating journey through the history of ancient Egypt during the time of the pharaohs. With more than 1,000 exhibits on display, including sarcophagi, mummies, jewelry, and amulets, the museum

107

offers a rich exploration of the life and traditions of this remarkable civilization.

Jordi Clos, a Spanish hotelier, collector, and patron, has long been captivated by the wonders of ancient Egyptian culture. In 1992, he decided to showcase around 70 of his archaeological treasures in an exhibition at the Hotel Claris in Barcelona. The exhibition drew substantial interest and received an overwhelmingly positive response. This led to the establishment of the Archaeological Foundation Clos, known as Fundació Arqueològica Clos. In 1994, the foundation opened the Egyptian Museum, which has since become home to over 1,100 exhibits, establishing itself as one of the foremost private collections from the time of the Pharaohs. Additionally, the museum has been housing the country's first school of Egyptology since 2000, further contributing to the study and appreciation of ancient Egypt.

- Getting There

To reach the Egyptian Museum, you can conveniently take the metro to Passeig de Gràcia station (L2, L3, L4). The museum is also accessible by the Bus Turístic, with the Casa Batlló - Fundació Antoni Tàpies stop nearby. If you prefer to drive, there are parking options available in the vicinity.

Art Galleries

Galeria Joan Prats

Since 1976, the Galeria has been displaying both well-known and up-and-coming artists. The gallery has a reputation for emphasizing conceptual art and new media.

Galeria Joan Prats is an art gallery located at Carrer Balmes, 54 in Barcelona, Spain. If you're interested in visiting, their opening hours are as follows: from Tuesday to Friday, they are open from 11am to 2pm and from 4pm to 8pm. On Saturdays, they are open from 11am to 2pm. Please note that they are closed on Mondays, except by appointment. It's important to mention that the gallery is closed during the month of August.

In addition to their main location, they also have a warehouse called Joan Prats Warehouse, which is situated at Passatge Saladrigas, 5 in Barcelona. If you wish to visit the warehouse, appointments are required.

To get in touch with Galeria Joan Prats, you can contact them via phone at +34 932 160 284 or through email at galeria@galeriajoanprats.com.

Fundació Suñol

A nonprofit organization that works to advance modern art in Barcelona. The gallery specializes in experimental art forms and exhibits work by both local and foreign artists.

For over four decades, Josep Suñol has been passionately expanding his collection by fostering relationships with artists, museum curators, gallery owners, and other art industry experts. This extensive network has allowed him to acquire artworks and develop a collection that not only represents his personal journey but also serves as a collective memory of the art world. The Suñol Soler Collection stands as a testament to the power of connections and the shared experiences that shape our appreciation of art.

You will find this organization at Carrer de Mejía Lequerica, 14, Barcelona Barcelona 08028 Spain

The Fundació Joan Miró's Espai 13

An experimental environment that prioritizes up-and-coming artists. A residence program for artists is also available at the gallery, which hosts many shows throughout the year.

ADN Galera

A gallery of modern art that exhibits a variety of modern pieces by Spanish and other artists. The gallery is renowned for emphasizing socially conscious art.

The Galería was established in 2003. This gallery has a distinct emphasis on thought-provoking works that not only reflect but also respond to the circumstances in which they were created. Beyond showcasing visual arts, the gallery places a strong emphasis on the interconnectedness of art, politics, and society. To foster this connection, ADN Galería organizes various events and activities through its "ADN Platform."

You can visit ADN Galeria from Monday to Friday, between 9:30 AM and 7:30 PM. On Saturdays, the gallery is open from 11:00 AM to 3:00 PM.

You can find ADN Galeria at C. Mallorca, 205 in Barcelona, Spain.

For more information, you can visit their website at http://www.adngaleria.com or contact them at +34 93 451 00 64.

N2 Galera

The hip Gràcia district is home to the N2 Galera, a gallery of contemporary art that exhibits the work of both well-known and up-and-coming artists. Contemporary photography is the gallery's main area of emphasis.

You can find N2 Galeria located at Enric Granados 61, 08008 Barcelona.

To contact the gallery, you can reach them at 93 452 0592.

The gallery is open from Monday to Friday with two separate time slots: 11am to 2pm and 5pm to 8:30pm. On Saturdays, visits are by appointment.

Feel free to visit N2 Galeria during their opening hours or schedule an appointment for a Saturday visit.

Galeria Valid Foto BCN

This photography gallery features the work of up-and-coming as well as seasoned photographers. Along with hosting numerous exhibitions throughout the year, the gallery also provides aspiring photographers with workshops and courses.

Galeria Valid Foto BCN is open with the following hours:

Tuesday to Friday: 10am to 2pm and 5pm to 8pm.

Saturday: 11am to 2pm.

Feel free to visit the gallery during their open hours to explore the exhibits and enjoy the artwork.

Architecture

Cases Godo-Lallana

Cases Godo-Lallana is a residential building that was designed by the talented architect Josep Maja i Ribas. Constructed between 1888 and 1890, this charming building features a unique chamfered design. One of its notable features is the presence of balconies on each floor, beautifully embellished with intricate wrought iron railings. The facade of the building is adorned with sgraffito, a decorative technique where colors and designs are etched onto the surface. An interesting detail is that the sgraffito on the top floor changes color, adding a touch of visual intrigue to the building's exterior.

Palau Montaner

Palau Montaner is an impressive early Modernist building located at the corner of Carrer Mallorca and Roger de Llúria, just off the vibrant Passeig de Gràcia. It exudes an Italianate charm that adds to its unique appeal.

Originally designed by Domenech i Estape, the construction of Ramon de Montaner's mansion was later completed by Montaner himself. On the facade, you'll find a mosaic that proudly displays the completion date, 1893, surrounded by intricate ornamental and symbolic motifs.

Step inside, and you'll be greeted by a magnificent grand staircase located in the central courtyard. Its stunning stained glass ceiling is truly a sight to behold. As you explore further, you'll notice the exquisite marble mosaics adorning the floors and the recesses filled with sculptures inspired by medieval art. Wooden panels with intricate overlays embellish the walls and ceilings, adding a touch of elegance and craftsmanship to the interior. Since 1980, Palau Montaner has served as the seat of the Spanish Government in Barcelona, adding historical and political significance to its architectural splendor.

If you're interested in experiencing Palau Montaner firsthand, mark the second day of each month on your calendar. On these special occasions, guided tours are available starting at 10:30 am and lasting approximately 90 minutes. To secure your spot, make sure to reserve at least 10 days in advance by calling 652 88 24 57. The tour fee is 12 euros per person.

113

Palau Montaner's address is Carrer de Mallorca, 278.

Casa Planells

Casa Planells, a remarkable architectural gem, was commissioned by Eveli Planells and designed by the esteemed Catalan Modernist architect Joseph Maria Jujol.

Constructed in 1924, this house stands out among other Modernist works in the Eixample district. It represents a culmination of two decades of Modernism, making it a significant architectural testament of its time.

The facade of Casa Planells is adorned with a captivating golden hue and features an irregular, undulating surface that adds a sense of uniqueness to the structure. Wooden blinds gracefully cover the windows, while both the windows and the entry door boast a rounded shape, adding an elegant touch to the overall design.

Inside, you'll find a captivating Modernist staircase crafted from intricately twisted wrought iron. While Casa Planells is not open to the public, it's worth taking a leisurely stroll past the house to appreciate the beauty of its facade and the artistic vision it embodies.

Casa Planells can be found at Avingude Diagonal, 332.

Mapfre Foundation in Casa Garriga Nogues

The Mapfre Foundation, owned by the insurance company Mapfre, is a private institution dedicated to promoting art. Its foundation-museum houses an impressive collection featuring works by renowned artists such as Monet, Renoir, and Rodin. In addition to its permanent collection, the foundation also hosts temporary art exhibitions, providing a dynamic cultural experience for visitors.

Beyond its remarkable art collection, the Mapfre Foundation is situated within the stunning Casa Garriga Nogues, an architectural gem located just a stone's throw away from the vibrant Passeig de Gracia. Designed by the talented architect Enric Sagnier, the building was constructed between 1899 and 1901 for the prominent banker Ruperto Garriga-Nogues.

The most notable feature of the Casa Garriga Nogues is its magnificent facade. Adorning the first floor is a protruding balcony, gracefully supported by four sculpted female figures created by Arnau. These sculptures symbolize the four stages of life, adding a touch of artistic symbolism to the building's exterior.

Stepping inside the house reveals a captivating interior, boasting elegant curving staircases, exquisite stained glass designed by Rigault, and meticulous attention to detail throughout.

You can find the Mapfre Foundation in Casa Garriga Nogues at Carrer de la Diputacio, 250. It's a must-visit destination for art enthusiasts and admirers of architectural beauty.

Museum of Catalan Modernism

If you're fascinated by Modernist architecture and design, then the Museum of Catalan Modernism, located in the Eixample neighborhood of Barcelona, is a must-visit destination. Eixample boasts the highest concentration of Modernist buildings in the city, making it the perfect setting for this museum.

Established in March 2010, the museum is relatively new but already houses an impressive collection of Modernist furniture, sculptures, and paintings. These valuable pieces were acquired from the private collections of two prominent antique dealers in Barcelona, ensuring their authenticity and significance.

One of the highlights of the museum is an entire room dedicated to the works of Antoni Gaudi, the renowned architect behind iconic structures such as Casa Calvet, Casa Batllo, and La Pedrera. Here, you can admire pieces designed by Gaudi himself, gaining a deeper appreciation for his distinctive style and innovative approach to architecture.

The Museum of Catalan Modernism is a treasure trove for lovers of architecture and design. It provides a comprehensive overview of Catalan Modernism, condensing its essence into one easily accessible location. Before your visit, make sure to check their website for any ongoing workshops or concerts,

116

which can add an extra layer of enrichment to your experience.

You can find the museum at Carrer de Balmes, 48. Prepare to be captivated by the beauty and artistic expression of Catalan Modernism in this immersive cultural institution.

Sant Pau Recinte Modernista

Also known as the Hospital of the Holy Cross and Saint Paul, this Montaner-designed hospital spans an impressive 10 city blocks. It's not your ordinary hospital; it's more like a theatrical masterpiece that celebrates the healing power of beauty. Patients here had the opportunity to nurture their souls along with their bodies.

Opening its doors in 1930, the Hospital de Sant Pau is conveniently located just a short 15-minute stroll from the Sagrada Família, down the vibrant Avenida de Gaudi. It was originally built as a philanthropic gesture by Pau Gil, who enlisted the popular architect Montaner for the project. Many consider this hospital to be Montaner's magnum opus.

In 1997, the hospital was rightfully recognized as a UNESCO World Heritage Site. It served as a fully functioning hospital until 2009, after which it underwent a restoration process that culminated in its reopening in 2014 as a museum and cultural center. Alongside Casa Vicens and Casa Amatller, it has quickly become one of Barcelona's newer and most captivating tourist attractions.

Prepare to be awestruck by the beauty that awaits you within the complex. The 27 intricately tiled pavilions appear almost as independent little cities within the larger cityscape. However, what's fascinating is that they are connected by underground tunnels, which you'll have the opportunity to explore during your visit.

Inside, the Main Hall will leave you spellbound. Its vaulted ceilings adorned with dazzling mosaics, intricate stone carvings, stained glass windows, and exquisite tiled domes create a mesmerizing visual spectacle. Every nook and cranny of the interior is meticulously crafted and deserves your admiration. And while you're there, don't miss the chance to relax at the street-level Cafe Vienes, where you can sip on cava while marveling at the vaulted ceiling and a forest of marble columns.

Make your way to Sant Antoni M. Claret, 167, and you'll find the entrance conveniently located on the corner of Carrer Dos de Maig.

Casa Batllo

Casa Batllo is one of the most extraordinary buildings you'll ever encounter. Antoni Gaudi's creativity was unleashed in full force here, delivering an out-of-this-world and dreamlike masterpiece.

Casa Batllo is a harmonious blend of grandeur and playfulness. Gaudi envisioned a structure that resembled a magnificent dragon, and the result is truly captivating. The facade, reminiscent of bones, demands your attention with its eerie skull mask balconies and a roof that undulates like the sinuous scales of a mythical creature.

Step closer to appreciate the intricate details of the mosaicked facade, a mesmerizing combination of blues, mauves, and greens. Despite its complexity, you'll notice the facade's gentle unevenness, resembling the calm undulations of a tranquil sea. It's as if the surface itself mimics the texture of a dragon's skin.

As you step inside Casa Batllo, you'll find yourself surrounded by a world of beauty. The interior is adorned with stunning tiles, sensuously curved wood, serpentine railings, and enchanting stained glass, all in organic shapes and forms. The motif feels like an ethereal underwater grotto, bathed in natural light streaming through skylights shaped like tortoise shells. The ceiling gracefully curves and bends, exuding a poetic allure.

Adding to the surrealistic ambiance, the humpback roof of Casa Batllo takes on a scaly appearance, reminiscent of a dragon or dinosaur. Its iridescent skin, adorned with raised spines, completes the mesmerizing composition.

Pay attention to the riotously colored Trencadis tiles, which symbolize the blood of the dragon's victims. And atop it all, the rooftop spire stands tall, representing the sword of St. George being thrust into the heart of the dragon.

119

Casa de les Punxes

Casa de les Punxes is a magnificent Modernist gem located in Barcelona, affectionately known as the House of Spikes. Designed by Puig i Cadafalch in 1905, this building stands out in the Eixample neighborhood as the only fully detached structure.

Prepare to be transported to a medieval world as you behold the impressive sight of Casa de les Punxes. Influenced by Germany's Neuschwanstein Castle, it exudes an air of grandeur and resembles a majestic fortress. The brick facade and roof immediately catch the eye, adorned with triangular pediments and crowned by six turrets that culminate in sharp spikes.

While the interior may not be as captivating as the exterior, there are still noteworthy features to appreciate. A graceful iron staircase, delicate floral motifs, and charming stained glass add to the overall charm. Don't miss the informative audiovisual display that tells the story of St. George and the Dragon, a significant symbol of Catalan Modernism.

Although privately owned, Casa de les Punxes opened its doors to the public in 2016, allowing visitors to marvel at its unique architecture. If you want to experience the full splendor of the pointy tile-adorned turrets up close, be sure to book a ticket that includes access to the root terrace.

During the summer, the terrace opens to the public on Friday nights, providing a rare opportunity to enjoy the enchanting views without the usual crowds. It's a perfect spot to soak up the atmosphere and admire the surroundings.

Make your way to Avinguda Diagonal, 420 to discover Casa de les Punxes, an architectural treasure that combines the beauty of Modernism with a touch of medieval allure.

La Pedrera

Welcome to Casa Mila, also known as La Pedrera, a UNESCO-listed masterpiece by Gaudi that showcases artistry both inside and out. This architectural marvel surpasses even Casa Batllo in terms of engineering brilliance, architectural design, and style, making it a true revolution in its time.

Initially met with disdain by the locals, Casa Mila earned the nickname "The Quarry" (or La Pedrera) due to its jagged, rocky facade and unconventional undulating shape. However, it has now rightfully claimed its place as one of the most treasured gems of the Catalan Art Nouveau movement.

The building evokes the image of a magnificent sea creature or a piece of coral sculpted by the gentle touch of the ocean. Following Gaudi's characteristic approach, Casa Mila draws inspiration from nature, particularly the elements of air, sea, and water. Its undulating form mimics the gentle waves and ripples of an enchanting ocean, while the intricately designed balconies resemble twisted kelp.

The moment you step inside, Casa Mila will captivate you. The tiled entrance courtyard welcomes you with the ambiance of

121

an underwater forest, setting the stage for the wonders that lie ahead. As you gaze upward, you'll be enchanted by the incredible views that reveal themselves. Light filters through the roof, casting an ethereal glow upon the interior apartments. Contrasting with the exterior's earthy hues, the interior unfolds as a mesmerizing marine wonderland with ceilings reminiscent of sea foam.

Venturing up to the iconic rooftop, you'll discover winding pathways and a forest of spiky chimneys numbering 30 in total. These chimneys, affectionately known as the "garden of warriors," bear a striking resemblance to the storm troopers from the renowned Star Wars films. Additionally, from the rooftop, you'll enjoy a delightful view of the magnificent Sagrada Familia.

In the evenings, Casa Mila transforms into an even more enchanting spectacle. A captivating audiovisual show takes place on the terrace, illuminating the rooftop and stairwells with mesmerizing projections set to music. You can savor this extraordinary performance while sipping a glass of cava, a delightful treat that is a package deal with your purchased ticket.

Music and theater

Known for its breathtaking modernista architecture, the **Palau de la Música Catalana** is a stunning music hall that is a UNESCO World Heritage Site. It's the ideal setting for taking in a concert of classical music.

Opera aficionados should not miss a trip to the **Gran Teatre del Liceu**, one of Europe's most prominent opera houses. With a gorgeous auditorium and classy furnishings, the structure itself is a work of art.

Teatre Lliure is a theater that specializes in modern Catalan play and is known for its cutting-edge and provocative performances.

Sala Apolo - For a fun night out, check out Sala Apolo for DJ sets and live music. From indie to electronic, the location presents a variety of genres.

Since the 1960s, Barcelona's music fans have enjoyed jazz performances at **Jamboree Jazz Club**, which is situated in the center of the Gothic Quarter. It's a nice place to unwind with some live music and a cocktail.

Beyoncé and U2 have both performed at the spacious sports and concert venue known as **Palau Sant Jordi**. It will undoubtedly be an unforgettable experience if you're fortunate enough to attend a concert here.

For clubgoers, **Razzmatazz** is a must-go location. Five distinct rooms are used for a variety of electronic, independent, and pop music events. Live music performances are frequently held there.

In the summer, a variety of performances are held in the open-air **Teatre Grec**, which is on Montjuic hill. For performances of theater, dance, and music, the location is lovely.

The modern concert venue **L'Auditori** presents a variety of classical and contemporary music concerts, as well as theater and dance productions. It's a fantastic location for seeing a show in a lovely environment.

Festivals and events

Primavera Sound Festival: Held in late May or early June, Primavera Sound is one of the most well-known music festivals in Europe. Both top international and local acts perform there.

Sant Jordi Day: Observed on April 23, is a day dedicated to love and literature. It's a day for buying and giving books to loved ones, as well as roses.

La Mercè Festival: This event honors the patron saint of Barcelona and is held in late September. It offers a variety of activities, such as concerts, parades, and fireworks.

Barcelona Beach Festival: This festival, which takes place in July and features prominent DJs from across the world, is a must-attend for fans of electronic dance music.

Grec Festival: At some of Barcelona's most recognizable venues, the Grec Festival presents theater, dance, and music acts every year from June through August.

Film Festival in Sitges: This festival, one of the best for fantasy and horror movies in the world, is only a short train trip from Barcelona.

Barcelona Beer Festival: Beer lovers gather at the Barcelona Beer Festival! This festival, which is held in May, showcases hundreds of specialty brews from different countries.

Festa Major de Gràcia: This neighborhood celebration, which takes place in February is known for its amazing display of hand-made street decorations.

International Jazz Festival: Jazz lovers won't want to miss this festival, which takes place in various locations throughout the city in October and November.

Sonar Festival: This festival, which takes place in June and involves both well-known and up-and-coming performers in the world of techno, house, and other electronic genres, is another essential for aficionados of electronic music.

Chapter Five

Food and Drink

Local Specialties

Paella

Paella is a traditional Spanish meal, and some of the best paellas in Spain can be found in Barcelona. For any culinary enthusiast, it is a must-try dish made with saffron-infused rice and a range of seafood and meats.

Crema Catalana

This creamy, caramelized delicacy has a Catalan flair but is similar to crème brûlée. It's the ideal way to cap off dinner because it's made with egg yolks, milk, sugar, and lemon zest.

Patatas Bravas

The crispy fried potatoes known as patatas bravas are a favorite snack in Barcelona. Usually, they come with aioli for dipping and a hot tomato sauce.

Escalivada

Roasted eggplant, red peppers, and onions are used to make this straightforward yet tasty recipe. It's frequently offered as a side dish or as a nice snack on top of toast.

Cava

Cava is a specialty of Catalonia and is the ideal beverage to serve with food or on special occasions. While having a similar conventional production process as champagne, it has a distinctive flavor profile.

Fideuà

Fideuà, similar to paella but prepared with short, thin noodles rather than rice, is a favorite. It usually contains seafood and is incredibly flavorful.

Churros

Churros are a traditional Spanish sweet made of fried dough. In Barcelona, they are frequently served with a rich, thick chocolate dipping sauce.

Butifarra

For meat enthusiasts, butifarra is a must-try sausage made in the Catalan way. It is typically served grilled or fried and is made with pork and a mixture of spices.

Coca de Recapte

This salty pastry is a favorite Barcelona snack. It is created from bread dough and topped with cheese, roasted veggies, and anchovies, among other things.

Gin and Tonic

Even though it's not cuisine, Barcelona's favorite cocktail, the gin, and tonic, deserves to be mentioned. Usually made with premium gin and garnished with unusual botanicals like juniper berries, rosemary, and orange peel.

Tapas Bars

To fully immerse yourself in the Barcelona experience, you should try tapas in at least one of these places:

The Poble Sec neighborhood's Quimet & Quimet: Noted for its mouthwatering montaditos (little sandwiches) and a wide variety of vermouth.

El Xampanyet: Situated in the hip El Born district, El Xampanyet is renowned for its traditional Catalan fare, which includes the typical patatas bravas and jamón ibérico.

Bar Canete: This well-known restaurant in the Gothic District offers a wide selection of traditional tapas meals, including croquettes, grilled octopus, and sizzling prawns.

Bar Mut: This classy, expensive tapas bar is ideal for a special date night. Unique items on their menu include truffle scrambled eggs and a selection of fine cheeses.

La Cova Fumada: This modest, family-run tapas restaurant in Barceloneta is renowned for creating the traditional dish known as "bomba," which is a potato croquette stuffed with hot meat. It continues to offer some of the best food in the area.

Restaurants

Fine Dining Restaurants

Barcelona provides many possibilities for people who want to savor some upscale cuisine. One of the top restaurants in the world, **El Celler de Can Roca** has three Michelin stars and a reputation for creating unique, original meals. **Tickets Bar**, with a focus on contemporary tapas and a colorful lively ambiance, is a must-visit if you're searching for something a little more conventional.

To immerse in Mediterranean cuisine, visit **Disfrutar** and try out their seafood menus. Then there's **Xera Restaurant** where you can try out mouthwatering Catalan dishes in a romantic setting. **Koy Shunka** serves Japanese cuisine in a chic atmosphere for diners who seek something different.

Budget Friendly Restaurants

Barcelona also offers a wide range of reasonably priced dining options for those who don't want to spend a lot on a meal. With kiosks selling everything from fresh seafood to cured meats and cheeses, **La Boqueria** market is a fantastic place to experience some of the greatest food in the city on a budget. Try **Bar Mut**, a tiny restaurant that serves straightforward but excellent cuisine created with fresh, local ingredients, for something a little more expensive but still within your budget. At **Tucco Real Food Eixample,** the food is great and the price is okay. Other budget friendly restaurants include: Toma Ya Street Food, La Taqueria(Mexican), Pizzeria Da Nanni Barcelona and Bar Xapako.

Vegan and Vegetarian Friendly Restaurants

There are numerous possibilities in Barcelona for vegetarians and vegans. While **Teresa Carles** is a well-liked regional brand that provides a variety of vegetarian and vegan cuisine, **Flax and Kale** is a trendy plant-based restaurant that serves great, healthful food in a stylish atmosphere. **Vegan Tulsi Restaurant** and **Vrutal** are great options, as well as **Bollywood Restaurant.**

Food markets

At least, one of Barcelona's thriving food markets is sure to have what you're searching for, whether you're seeking locally produced fruits and vegetables, cured meats, cheeses, or fresh seafood.

La Boqueria is one of the city's most well-known marketplaces, and it's just off Las Ramblas. It's easy to understand why this ancient market has long been a mainstay of the city's culinary scene. La Boqueria provides everything, from exotic fruits and vegetables to fresh seafood. The market's mouthwatering empanadas, seafood paella, and freshly squeezed juices are well worth trying.

Visit the **Mercat de la Barceloneta** in the quaint seaside community of Barceloneta if you want a more authentic experience. Fresh seafood is a feature of this market, and it also serves fideuà, a paella-like meal made with short noodles in place of rice.

Visit the **Mercat de Sant Antoni** in the developing area of Sant Antoni if you wish to go off the beaten path. Together with its hip bars and eateries, this market is renowned for its excellent range of cured meats, cheeses, and organic veggies.

Cooking Classes and Food tours

Cook & Taste: This well-known cooking school offers courses on everything from the fundamentals of Spanish cooking to more complex, multi-course dinners. In a laid-back, welcoming setting, you will learn from seasoned chefs and then get to enjoy the results of your labor with a glass of wine.

La Boqueria Market Tour & Cooking Class: This tour will lead you through La Boqueria's vibrant stalls, one of Barcelona's most well-known food markets, before bringing you to a neighboring kitchen for a practical cooking lesson. You'll discover how to prepare Catalan cuisine staples like paella and crema catalana. Several companies offer this tour online and you can check and choose the best tour to suit you.

Tip: To skip the line and jump queues, it is always best to book in advance from reputable companies.

132

Devour Barcelona: Devour Barcelona offers a selection of food tours that highlight various localities and culinary subcultures. The best tapas bars, the hippest gastronomy scene, or the city's hidden gems may all be discovered on different trips. Each trip includes some stops and mouth watering sampling.

Spanish Culinary Experience: This family-run cooking school offers classes in everything from paella to churros, with a focus on traditional Spanish food. With seasoned chefs, you'll discover the secrets of Spanish home cuisine before sitting down to eat the meal you made.

Tapas and wine are two of Spain's greatest pleasures, and they are combined on this tour. While learning about the history and culture of the Catalan capital, you'll visit a selection of genuine tapas places and savor the finest local wines.

Chapter Six

Outdoor Activities

Beaches

Barceloneta Beach

Barceloneta Beach has emerged as the go-to beach destination in Barcelona, capturing the hearts of tourists from all over the world. This vibrant beach underwent a transformation for the 1992 Olympic Games, propelling it into the global spotlight. Conveniently located near the city center, it offers easy accessibility not only to the sandy shores but also to the lively beach bars and clubs that contribute to Barcelona's renowned nightlife. Barceloneta Beach is a place that never sleeps, buzzing with activity both day and night. While it may not boast untouched white sands and crystal-clear waters, it compensates with its lively atmosphere and the opportunity to immerse oneself in the city's tourist culture. It's also a convenient landing spot for those who have enjoyed a night out at one of the popular bars nearby. As you approach Barceloneta Beach, you'll be greeted by the iconic fish statue by Frank Gehry, known as El Peix, which stands as a landmark at the beach's border.

It's the ideal location for a day of sun, sea, and sand thanks to its golden sand, lively atmosphere, and several seaside restaurants and pubs.

Nova Mar

If you're seeking a peaceful beach right within Barcelona, head to Nova Mar. While it might take a bit longer to reach, the tranquility and serene atmosphere make it worth the journey. This hidden gem is perfect for those looking to relax on the sandy shores and immerse themselves in a good book. Located just a twenty-minute walk from the Selva de Mar stop, Nova Mar is also conveniently close to the Diagonal Mar shopping center, renowned for its fantastic shopping options. After enjoying some sun and surf, you can easily head over to the shopping center to grab a bite to eat or enjoy refreshing drinks. Nova Mar offers the ideal combination of peaceful beach vibes and proximity to urban conveniences, making it a wonderful choice for a laid-back beach day in Barcelona.

Playa De Bogatell

Bogatell Beach is a more tranquil and family-friendly alternative to Barceloneta and is located in the Poble Nou area. The beach is large and has room for volleyball, beach volley, and other beach activities.

Located between Nova Icaria and Barceloneta, it offers a refreshing alternative with fewer crowds compared to its neighboring beaches. Despite being conveniently close to two metro stops, it maintains a relatively peaceful atmosphere. This makes Bogatell an excellent choice for families seeking a relaxed beach experience. The waters here are known to be relatively clean and shallow for a significant stretch, making it a safe and enjoyable swimming spot, particularly for young children and those who are not confident swimmers. If you're feeling more adventurous, you'll also find tour operators offering paddleboard and kite surfing lessons for those eager to venture farther out into the sea. Bogatell Beach provides a balanced mix of tranquility and opportunities for exciting water activities.

Playa De la Mar Bella

If you want a less hectic and crowded choice, go to Mar Bella. Locals frequent this beach because of its nudist section and calm, swimming-friendly waves.

It is nicely tucked away and reachable from the Llacuna metro stop, and offers a more secluded experience. A leisurely 15-minute walk behind a sand dune will lead you to this hidden gem. Mar Bella is renowned for being the most nude-friendly beach in Barcelona, attracting a diverse crowd who enjoy sunbathing au naturel. However, it's important to note that you'll also find plenty of people sporting speedos, bikinis, and boardshorts, so there's no pressure for those who prefer a more modest approach. Mar Bella Beach has a reputation for being inclusive and welcoming to the LGBTQ+ community, making it known as the gay-friendliest beach in the area. Whether you choose to embrace the freedom of clothing-optional sunbathing or simply relax in your swimwear, Mar Bella offers a laid-back and open-minded atmosphere for all to enjoy.

Ocata Beach

A broad, open beach with excellent waters that is situated in the village of El Masnou. It's a fantastic alternative for people who wish to get away from the city's bustle.

Ocata Beach is just a short half-hour train ride from the city, its a hidden gem known for its tranquil atmosphere and stunning golden-white sand. Renowned as the most beautiful beach in Barcelona, Ocata offers a peaceful and serene getaway, away from the hustle and bustle of the city center.

Couples seeking privacy or anyone looking for a quieter beach experience will find Ocata to be the perfect destination. It's a place where you can unwind, relax, and enjoy the beauty of the surroundings. Additionally, there are nearby sightseeing options such as the historic Iglesia de Sant Pere, the oldest surviving parish church in the vicinity of Ocata Beach.

Stretching out with its long and wide shoreline, Ocata Beach provides ample space for visitors to bask in the sun and enjoy the beach. As it attracts fewer tourists compared to other beaches, there may be fewer dining and entertainment options in the immediate area. However, by exploring the surroundings, you can still discover charming beachside eateries known as "chiringuitos" where you can savor fresh seafood dishes and sip on refreshing drinks.

Castelldefels Beach

This is a popular location for water sports like windsurfing and kitesurfing. It is a long, sandy beach that is located just outside of Barcelona. There are several fantastic coastal restaurants and pubs there as well.

Sant Sebastià Beach

Sant Sebestia, located on the eastern end of the city, holds the title of being both the oldest and longest beach in Barcelona. It's actually a part of Sitges, a charming town known for its abundance of 17 beaches, making it an excellent destination for a weekend trip from Barcelona. If you're seeking a vibrant atmosphere without being overwhelmed by crowds, Sant Sebestia strikes the perfect balance. This beach caters to different preferences, as it is nudist-friendly and also accessible for individuals with disabilities.

Sports enthusiasts will be delighted by the fantastic facilities available at Sant Sebestia. From volleyball courts to a wide range of extreme sports, there's something for everyone to enjoy. While the beach does attract a fair share of tourists, you'll also spot many locals who frequent this iconic spot.

Compared to the bustling Barceloneta Beach, Sant Sebestia offers a more relaxed and less crowded experience, making it ideal for swimming. The atmosphere exudes tranquility, with paddleboarders and sailboats gracefully gliding along the horizon. And of course, there's no shortage of dining options available right on the sand, ensuring that you can satisfy your hunger while soaking up the sun.

Some other beaches include:

- Cala Fonda Beach

Cala Fonda is a picturesque cove encircled by cliffs and pine trees and is situated in the nearby town of Tarragona. Although getting there requires a little bit of hiking, the breathtaking scenery and pure waters are well worth the effort.

- Caldetes Beach

A quaint, little beach in the village of Caldes d'Estrac that is well-known for its tranquil waves and picturesque surroundings. It's the ideal location for a serene beach day.

- Garraf Beach

This hidden gem is located in the Garraf Natural Park and is well worth the trip. It's the ideal location for a tranquil day of swimming and sunbathing with its crystal-clear waters and breathtaking views.

- Cala del Mago

A hidden cove in the neighboring town of Sitges that's ideal for a romantic break. It's the ideal place to get away from the crowds and enjoy some peace because it is surrounded by cliffs and lakes that are stunningly clear.

Hiking and Nature parks

Montserrat

Montserrat, located around 30 km from Barcelona in Spain, is an impressive mountain range that offers a popular day trip from the city. It is not only a place of pilgrimage but also a favorite spot for hiking, similar to Vall de Nuria.

The breathtaking mountain range is only a short train journey from Barcelona.

The name "Montserrat" translates to "serrated mountain" in Catalan, perfectly capturing the sharp-toothed nature of the peaks. Their vertical ascent from the plains makes them easily recognizable from a distance.

The mountain range of Montserrat consists of several peaks, with the highest one, Saint Jerome, reaching 1,236 meters above sea level. The mountains stand out dramatically from the surrounding landscape, characterized by their jagged and saw-like appearance. One of the main attractions of Montserrat is the **Benedictine Abbey**, founded in the 11th century, which sits 718 meters up the mountain. The abbey houses a significant Roman Catholic relic, a **Statue of the Madonna and Child** believed to date back to at least the 12th century. This has made Montserrat a significant pilgrimage site for centuries.

Montserrat is approximately 20 miles (30 kilometers) northwest of Barcelona. The driving distance is around 40 miles (65 kilometers), making it easily accessible for a day trip. Various transportation options from Barcelona to Montserrat take about an hour to 90 minutes.

The closest town to Montserrat is **Monistrol de Montserrat**, located at the foot of the mountain on the east side. The nearest city is Manresa, situated slightly to the north.

You can visit Montserrat at any time of year, but keep in mind that the mountain's elevation affects the temperature and weather. It tends to be cooler and windier compared to the surrounding areas, and fog is common. While snow is rare, it can happen during winter months.

In summer, average temperatures range from 23°C/73°F to 29°C/84°F, while in winter, they range from 9°C/48°F to 15°C/59°F. These are just averages, so temperatures can vary.

For hiking, spring and autumn offer a good balance of pleasant weather and comfortable temperatures. Keep in mind that weekends, especially Sundays, are the busiest times to visit, so if possible, try to avoid those days for a quieter experience.

Practical Information

Taking Photos

While you are allowed to take photos at most locations in Montserrat, there are a few exceptions and rules to follow.

- In the Basilica interior, photography is allowed except during religious services. Flash photography and the use of tripods are not permitted.
- At the Montserrat Museum, flash photography and tripods are not allowed, and some temporary exhibitions may have photography restrictions.

You don't need to purchase tickets to see the Basilica at Montserrat, and you can freely explore the church and see the Black Madonna Statue without any charge.

However, there are opportunities to leave a donation, and you can also purchase a candle to light.

Keep in mind that there are fees for visiting the museums and using various transportation options on the mountain.

There is no official luggage storage at Montserrat. If you're staying at a hotel, you can usually leave your luggage at the reception before or after checkout and retrieve it when needed.

It's advisable to avoid bringing large bags to the mountain, as some attractions like the museum don't allow entry with large bags.

Prohibited items: Food, drinks, bags, firearms, umbrellas, knives, and similar items are not permitted in most buildings. Devices like electric scooters and skateboards are also not allowed, except for those required for mobility purposes.

Pets, specifically dogs, are allowed on the hiking trails and outdoor areas of Montserrat but are not allowed inside the Basilica, museums, or other indoor areas. Dogs must be kept on a leash at all times.

If you plan to bring your dog on the rack railway or cable car, it must be muzzled and on a leash. Smaller animals should be in a basket or cage. Please note that dogs are allowed on the train from Barcelona.

Getting To Montserrat

When it comes to traveling from Barcelona to Montserrat, you have several options to choose from. You can drive, take public transport, cycle, or join a guided tour. Here's a breakdown of each option:

- By Driving

If you have a car, driving to Montserrat is a straightforward option. The journey from Barcelona city center to the mountain area where you can park takes a little over an hour, depending on traffic. Simply follow the C-31 road northeast out of Barcelona, then take the C-58 northwest to Montserrat.

Once you reach the town of Monistrol de Montserrat, you have two choices for reaching the monastery. You can continue driving up the steep and winding road until you reach the parking area near the top of the mountain. From there, it's a 10 to 20-minute walk to the monastery. The parking area is free for the first 30 minutes, and then it costs €6.50 per day.

Alternatively, you can park in Monistrol de Montserrat and take either the Montserrat rack railway (Cremallera de Montserrat) or the Aeri de Montserrat cable car. Both options offer free parking. The rack railway ticket prices vary depending on the time of year and your age, while the cable car costs €7.50 for a one-way trip and €11.50 for a return journey.

- By Train

It takes approximately an hour to reach the town of Monistrol de Montserrat at the base of the mountain by train. From there, you can continue your journey by taking the rack railway or cable car to the top.

The R5 train to Manresa is the one you need to catch from Barcelona-Plaça Espanya Station. Trains run regularly, approximately every half hour, starting around 9:30 am. You can check the train schedule on the FGC website. At the station, you can purchase combined train tickets that include the return rack railway or cable car ticket. Make sure to allow enough time for your visit, considering the transportation time and the schedule of the rack railway or cable car.

It's worth noting that if you have a Barcelona discount pass that includes transportation, such as a Barcelona Pass or Barcelona Card, the transportation does not cover the entire journey to Montserrat. You will need to buy separate train tickets.

Choosing the right ticket option:

When purchasing tickets at the Barcelona-Plaça Espanya Station, you can choose between different combinations that include the train journey and either the rack railway or cable car. Automated ticket vending machines are available, and they are often the preferred option for the basic return ticket. The manned ticket booths primarily sell higher-priced combination tickets with more inclusions.

It's important to decide in advance whether you want to take the cable car or rack railway, as the type of transport will determine which train station you get off at. For the cable car, you should get off at the Aeri de Montserrat stop, while for the rack railway, you should alight at the Monistrol de Montserrat stop.

Keep in mind that the train back to Barcelona can get crowded, and you might end up standing. If this is a concern, it's better to opt for the funicular rack railway, as it's the first stop for the Montserrat stations the train stops at.

Regardless of the transportation option you choose, the journey to Montserrat offers breathtaking views and a memorable experience.

Other Ticket Options

In addition to the basic combination tickets for train and cable car or train and funicular, there are other ticket options available that offer additional services and inclusions. These tickets can be purchased in advance to save time at the train station or online through the Barcelona Tourism website.

When buying tickets online, you will need to exchange the voucher for the actual tickets. You can collect your tickets at various locations, including the tourist information point in Plaça Catalunya, the tourist information point in Barcelona Airport, and the FGC (Catalan Rail) station in plaça Espanya.

Let's take a look at the different ticket choices and what they offer:

- Tot Montserrat:

This is the most expensive ticket, but it includes several features that can be cost-effective if you take advantage of them. In addition to the return train journey and your choice of cable car or funicular transport, it includes a round-trip metro ticket within Barcelona, unlimited rides on the Sant Joan funicular, entrance to the Montserrat audiovisual exhibit, admission to the Museu de Montserrat, and a meal in the self-service restaurant at Montserrat. If you plan on spending the whole day at Montserrat, this ticket offers great value and convenience.

146

- **Trans Montserrat**:

This ticket is slightly more expensive than the basic combination ticket. Along with the return train journey and round-trip cable car or funicular transport, it includes a round-trip metro ticket within Barcelona, unlimited rides on the Sant Joan funicular, and entrance to the Montserrat audiovisual exhibit. The inclusion of the Sant Joan funicular alone makes this ticket worthwhile.

- Montserrat Exprés:

This special service guarantees you a seat on the train departing from Plaça España. It includes the return train journey, funicular transport up the mountain, an audioguide in 8 languages, a guide to the shrine of Montserrat, a box of carquinyolis (hard almond biscuits) from Montserrat, a tasting of typical liqueurs, and a pack of discounts for different services. If the idea of a guaranteed seat and the additional add ons appeal to you, this is a good option.

These combination tickets can be used for an overnight stay, but all the included parts (funicular, meal, monastery, etc.) must be used on the first day. It's advisable to check with the Barcelona Tourism office for any changes or updates before planning an overnight stay.

By Bus

There is a direct bus service operated by Autocares Julia that departs once a day from Barcelona to the top area of Montserrat. The bus departs from Estación de Autobuses de Barcelona/Sants, which is next to Sants Train Station on Viriat

Street, approximately a 10-minute walk from Plaça Espanya. Although online booking is not available, this is one of the most affordable options at just over €5 each way, and the journey takes about 90 minutes.

Alternatively, you can book a tour that includes round-trip bus transport only. These tours are slightly more expensive but allow you to book in advance and ensure a smooth experience.

- By Cycling

For adventurous and experienced cyclists, it is possible to bike from Barcelona to Montserrat, but keep in mind that it's a challenging route of approximately 145 kilometers round trip with steep climbs. We recommend this option only for fit and capable cyclists with experience in similar trips. Several companies offer bike rentals and route planning assistance, and some even provide guided tours for added support.

- Guided Tours

Taking a guided tour is one of the most popular and convenient ways to visit Montserrat from Barcelona. Simply book a tour, show up at the departure point (or wait for the hotel pickup, if available), and enjoy the scenic journey and sights. Tour prices and inclusions vary, but they generally include round-trip transportation to/from Barcelona, time to explore Montserrat, and transportation up the mountain, which may be by bus or rack railway.

Some tours offer additional features such as sightseeing in the area, food, wine tasting, museum entry, and more. The duration of tours typically ranges from half a day to a full day, depending on the inclusions.

We recommend selecting a tour based on your interests, desired inclusions, and budget. It's also a good idea to read recent reviews from other travelers when choosing a tour.

Getting Around Montserrat

Once you reach the top of Montserrat via cable car, rack railway, or car, you can easily explore the area on foot. The monastery, main restaurants, and shops are all located at the same level.

The Basilica entrance is situated one level above, accessible either by walking up a slope or using a staircase, equivalent to about four flights of stairs.

At this level, you'll also find the Sant Joan Funicular and the Santa Cova funicular, which serve different parts of the mountain. The stations for these funiculars are close to each other and in proximity to the cable car and rack railway stations.

The Sant Joan funicular takes you from the monastery level up to an altitude above 1,000 meters. The ride offers breathtaking views (although it can be a bit nerve-wracking for those afraid of heights), and from the top, there are various hiking trails across the mountain.

The Santa Cova funicular descends to the cave where, according to legend, shepherds discovered the image of the

Virgin Mary, now housed in the Basilica. This area is a popular pilgrimage site and features sculptures by Catalan artists, including Gaudi. The lower Santa Cova funicular station also houses a small museum about Santa Cova and funiculars in general.

Both of these locations can also be reached by foot. The hike up to Sant Joan takes approximately 45 minutes to an hour each way, while the hike down to Santa Cova is around 20-30 minutes each way. Opting for the funiculars will save you time and energy.

Keep in mind that the funiculars may occasionally be closed for maintenance or other reasons. You can check the current status on the official website.

Montserrat Bucket List

- Visit the Aula Natura Exhibit and Hike Down:

Explore the Aula Natura exhibition at the top of the Sant Joan Funicular. Learn about the history, geology, flora, and fauna of Montserrat. Take a hike downhill for fantastic views.

- Visit the Espai Audiovisual Museum

Experience a multimedia exhibition that delves into the history, geology, and cultural aspects of Montserrat. Watch a video presentation on the monastery's daily life.

- Go Hiking

Explore the hiking trails in Montserrat, ranging from easy walks to full-day hikes. Pick up a hiking map from the Tourist

Information Office or check the official website for suggested routes.

- Go Climbing:

If you're an experienced climber, Montserrat offers over 1,000 climbing routes of varying levels. Get advice from the Tourist Information Office on climbing areas and routes.

- Visit the Santa Maria de Montserrat Abbey

Explore the abbey, including the basilica and the museum. Don't miss the famous statue of the Virgin of Montserrat, Catalonia's patron saint.

- Explore Monistrol de Montserrat

This is the town at the foot of the mountain. There are historical landmarks, including a 14th-century bridge, defensive towers, and a 16th-century aqueduct. Take a stroll around the town center to experience its charm.

- Visit the Museum of Montserrat:

Discover the impressive art collections, including works by renowned artists like Dali, Monet, Chagall, Picasso, and Miro. The museum also showcases archaeological exhibits.

- Listen to the Escolania de Montserrat (Boys' Choir) Perform:

Attend a performance by one of Europe's oldest boys choirs, known as the Escolania de Montserrat. Check the schedule for their performances in the Basilica.

- Ride the Rack Railway / Cable Car:

Enjoy the scenic views by taking the rack railway or cable car up and down the mountain. Consider riding them for the experience alone or combined with hiking.

- Visit St. Michael's Cross:

Take a walk to St. Michael's Cross, starting near the Santa Cova funicular station. Enjoy breathtaking views of the monastery and surrounding mountains.

- Go Sightseeing

Discover additional activities, workshops, and events taking place at Montserrat. Visit the Monestir de Sant Benet de Montserrat and explore the hermitages and smaller churches.

Where to Stay on Montserrat

Abat Oliba Hostel: Budget-friendly hostel accommodation, including dormitories and private rooms for solo travelers, couples, and families.

Hotel Abat Cisneros: A 3-star hotel located next to the Basilica, offering comfortable rooms and stunning views.

Abat Marcet Apartments: Serviced apartments with kitchen facilities, suitable for longer stays or those who prefer apartment-style accommodation.

Enjoy your visit to Montserrat and make the most of these incredible experiences!

Camping on Montserrat:

There is a small campsite located on the trail up to the Creu de Sant Miquel, about 10 minutes from the monastery. It is primarily for climbers but open to anyone looking for a campsite. It is for tent camping only and reached by foot.

The cost is around €10 per adult + about €5 per person. The site cannot be booked in advance and is only open for check-in between 5pm and 8pm. It is primarily open during the main season and closed over winter.

You need to bring your own camping equipment, but there are toilets, showers, wash basins, and a small kitchen area with a fridge available.

Tips for Visiting Montserrat:

Avoid crowds by visiting early in the morning or staying late in the evening. Start with the most popular places like the Basilica and the Statue of the Virgin, followed by the funicular to the top of the mountain.

Consider staying overnight to explore more and experience a peaceful environment. Most visitors leave by 5pm, and you can enjoy the place by yourself, catch the sunrise and sunset, and witness the early light hitting the monastery buildings.

Dress appropriately for the religious location, covering shoulders and knees. Also, bring warm layers as it can be cooler and windier on the mountain than the surrounding plains. Proper hiking or climbing gear is essential for outdoor activities.

Also, it is highly recommended to see the renowned Montserrat Abbey with its exquisite church and magnificent art collection.

Parc Natural de la Serra de Collserola

Parc Natural de la Serra de Collserola, spanning over 8,000 hectares, is an oasis of greenery nestled in the midst of one of the most densely populated urban areas along the Mediterranean coast. It serves as a prominent natural boundary that separates the city from its surrounding towns, preventing endless urban sprawl.

Beyond its role as a buffer zone, the park is a precious natural and ecological treasure. It brings together two distinct climatic worlds: the Euro-Siberian and the Mediterranean, resulting in a diverse landscape mosaic. Within its boundaries, you'll encounter forests of Aleppo pines and nut pines, evergreen oak woodlands, riverside groves, scrublands, and grassy savannas. Over 1,000 plant species have been cataloged in the park, creating an environment that supports a rich and varied wildlife population. From genets, and stone martens to rabbits, and squirrels, the park is teeming with interesting animals. Bird enthusiasts will be delighted by the wide range of bird species, including blue tits, whitethroats, tree creepers, woodpeckers, as well as birds of prey like the goshawk and sparrow hawk.

Despite the incredible biodiversity and ecological value of Collserola, many city residents have yet to explore its wonders. The park's uphill position relative to the city requires more effort to reach compared to the beach. However, for those willing to venture into its depths, Collserola offers its own rewards. Whether you're an avid mountain biker, a history enthusiast drawn to its medieval heritage, or a star gazer captivated by its dark skies, the park will intrigue you.

Within the park, there are several facilities where you can find information about the various activities and routes available. These include the information centre, as well as the environmental education centres of Mas Pins and Can Coll, and the documentation and educational resources centre.

Along with these resources, the park features a network of signposted routes that guide you through its beautiful landscapes. You'll come across recreational areas, viewpoints, and even natural springs, such as the popular Budellera spring. One of the iconic landmarks in the park is the renowned Collserola tower, a stunning architectural masterpiece designed by Norman Foster. Standing at a height of 288 meters, it offers an incredible vantage point to enjoy panoramic views of the Barcelona plain. It's a must-visit spot for capturing breathtaking vistas of the surrounding area.

The Collserola Information Centre offers a variety of nature trails and guided activities within the park, including special stargazing nights. These events are a great way to get acquainted with observing the night sky. You'll have the opportunity to learn about stars, planets, and the fascinating myths associated with them. The activities combine theoretical explanations with the practical experience of watching the sky in the open air. You'll have the chance to identify constellations both with the naked eye and through the use of a telescope. It's a wonderful way to deepen your understanding of the cosmos and appreciate the beauty of the night sky.

- Getting There
- By Train

If you're planning to reach the Park by train, you can hop on the Ferrocarrils de la Generalitat de Catalunya (FGC) at several stations.

These include Baixador de Vallvidrera, les Planes, la Floresta, Valldoreix, and Sant Cugat. Another option is to take the Funicular de Vallvidrera from the Peu de Funicular station. These transportation options provide convenient access to the Park, allowing you to easily explore its natural beauty and enjoy all that it has to offer.

- By Subway

You can take the TMB metro line 11, which runs between Trinitat Nova and Can Cuiàs. Alternatively, you can hop on the TMB metro line 3, which connects Zona Universitària and Trinitat Nova. These subway lines provide convenient access to the park, making it easy for you to embark on your Collserola adventure.

- By Rodalies Renfe Trains

If you're planning to reach the park using the Rodalies Renfe trains, you have several station options located in the nearby towns.

You can catch the train at stations in Papiol, Molins de Rei, Sant Feliu de Llobregat, Torre Baró, and Cerdanyola del Vallès. These train stations provide convenient access to the park, allowing you to easily embark on your Collserola adventure.

- By Public Transport

Barcelona's public transport network operated by Transport Metropolità de Barcelona (TMB) is a convenient and reliable way to reach the park. Numerous bus lines are available, making it easy to access various parts of the natural park. Whether you're looking to explore the park's trails, visit specific landmarks, or simply enjoy the natural beauty, hopping on a TMB bus is a great option. You can rely on the extensive bus network to take you to different areas of the park, ensuring a seamless and enjoyable journey.

Collserola Bucket List

- Explore the Temple Expiatori del Sagrat Cor

The Collserola area is brimming with exciting attractions and beckons you to embark on nature hikes. Just on the Barcelona side, you'll encounter the Tibidabo mountain range. At its summit, you'll discover an amusement park and the Temple Expiatori del Sagrat Cor.

- Explore the Amusement Park on Tibidabo

Parc Tibidabo is one of the world's oldest operating amusement parks, dating back to 1905. It still retains many of its original attractions, offering a nostalgic experience.

The church atop the mountain was constructed between 1902 and 1962 and has been bestowed the title of Basilica Minor by Pope John XXIII.

- Ascend Barcelona's Telecom Tower

A hidden gem awaits you as you ascend the Torre de Collserola, Barcelona's iconic telecom tower designed by Sir Norman Foster. This emblematic tower was built for the 1992 Olympic Games and boasts a futuristic design. From its glass elevator, you'll enjoy breathtaking views from the observation deck. On clear days, you can even see as far as the mountain monastery of Montserrat. The telecom tower remains one of the few attractions in Barcelona that has yet to be overrun by tourists.

- Experience the Carretera de les Aigües – Barcelona's Scenic Pathway

By taking public transport from downtown Barcelona and then switching to the funicular at Peu de Funicular, you can disembark at the mid-stop and embark on a stroll along the Carretera de les Aigües – the waterway. This trail derived its name from the water pipes that used to run alongside it. Offering magnificent viewpoints from the Collserola ridge overlooking the entirety of Barcelona, this nearly 10-kilometer path, with its highest point reaching 300 meters above sea level, has become a popular choice among locals for cycling and walking.

- Go Hiking in Collserola

The natural park provides an array of hiking options, complete with resting spots and picnic areas. You can easily traverse the entire park in any direction and then conveniently take the train back to Barcelona. Alternatively, you can plan a circular hiking route, allowing you to immerse yourself fully in the park's natural beauty.

Psst: Download the AllTrails App to find the best trails that suit your preference.

Parc del Laberint d'Horta

This lovely garden with a hedge labyrinth that's ideal for a stroll is another fantastic location for nature enthusiasts. It is a tranquil sanctuary in the center of the city with its fountains, waterfalls, and sculptures.

Parc del Laberint, spanning 9.1 hectares, came under the ownership of the city of Barcelona in 1967 and has been open to the public since 1971. This hidden gem also doubles as a botanical museum, showcasing its rich collection of plant species. In 1994, the park underwent restoration to preserve its historical and natural beauty.

Located off the beaten tourist path, Parc del Laberint offers a serene and tranquil escape that can be hard to find within the bustling city of Barcelona. As the oldest remaining park in Barcelona, it was originally created in the 18th century by the Marquis Desvall for the Catalan nobility. The park features a charming castle, inspired by Moorish architecture, known as the Palais of the Desvalls family.

To reach the park using public transport, you can take the metro and enjoy a short walk from the Mundet station (line L3). With the Barcelona Card, you can even enjoy free access to public transportation, including your journey to the park. The Parc del Laberint is divided into two sections: the traditional park and the romantic garden.

As you explore the park, starting from the castle, you'll encounter three terraces adorned with classical elements, sculptures, streams, and ponds. The highlight of the park is the labyrinth, established in 1792, with its meticulously trimmed cypress hedges spanning approximately 750 meters. Within the labyrinth, you'll find a statue of the huntress Diana and Cupid, offering an enchanting experience for visitors.

Moving through the park, you'll discover two small temples dedicated to Artemis and Danae, as well as a statue of Dionysus near the stairs to the third terrace. The third and uppermost terrace features a pavilion honoring the nine

Muses, accompanied by a water basin and fountain dedicated to the nymph Egeria.

In the late 19th century, the descendants of the Marquis Desvalls expanded the park, adding a delightful Romanesque garden filled with shaded paths and large trees. This section also includes a replica of a medieval cemetery, offering a contrasting experience to the classical part of the park.

Set within a vast Mediterranean forest on the slope of Collserola, near the Olympic bicycle stadium, Parc del Laberint is a peaceful haven. From the Mundet metro station, it's a walk of about 500 meters uphill to reach the park, allowing you to immerse yourself in nature as you ascend the slope.

Tickets and Hours

Please note that a maximum of 750 people are allowed inside the Parc del Laberint at the same time to ensure a pleasant experience for visitors. The park is open from 10:00 in the morning until dusk.

For admission, the normal ticket price is €2.17, while a reduced ticket is available for €1.38. Children under 5 years old and pensioners can enjoy free admission. Additionally, on Wednesdays and Sundays, entrance to the park is free of charge for all visitors.

Water sports

Jet Skiing:

Enjoy the rush of gliding across the waves of the Mediterranean Sea on a jet ski. Many jet ski rental businesses in Barcelona provide guided trips down the shore where you can take in the breathtaking views of the city skyline.

Parasailing:

Have a parasailing trip to soar over the Mediterranean Sea. You'll get a bird's-eye view of the gorgeous Barcelona shoreline from this heart-pounding adventure. Lift off from the shore while being towed by a speedboat, then soar high over the water.

Stand-up Paddleboarding (SUP):

The calm seas close to the Barceloneta beach are ideal for SUP. Take in the sights and sounds of the city's coastline while paddling in tranquility.

Windsurfing:

Barcelona is a popular location for windsurfing because of the city's reliable winds. Visit the Platja de Sant Sebastià, one of the city's most well-liked windsurfing locations, to get the wind in your sails.

Kayaking:

Explore the city's coastline by kayak and find undiscovered coves and isolated beaches. Kayaking is a fantastic opportunity to get a terrific workout while experiencing the city from a new angle.

Kitesurfing:

Kitesurfing may be the ideal option for individuals seeking an adventurous water sports activity. A well-liked location for

162

kitesurfing is Castelldefels, a town outside of Barcelona, because of its beaches' reputation for high winds.

Water Sports Operators in Barcelona

- Moloka'i SUP Center Barceloneta: Offers Private Sup Lessons for Beginners, stand up paddle boarding lessons For Beginners. They have equipments available
- Sea Riders Badalona: Offering Jet ski Lessons

This list is not exhaustive and there are plenty of options, so you will find something that's right for you.

Cycling

Barcelona is a city of many wonders, and riding a bike is one of the greatest ways to discover them all. Several riding trails in and around the city offer breathtaking views, historical landmarks, and an opportunity to get some exercise while experiencing the local culture, whether you're an experienced cyclist or just getting started.

The Carretera de les Aigües, or "Road of the Waters," is one of Barcelona's most well-known bicycle routes. You will traverse Collserola Mountains on this trail, which provides amazing views of the city skyline and the Mediterranean Sea. Families or anyone going for a more leisurely ride will find the path to be an excellent alternative because it is primarily flat.

The Montserrat Mountains provide some of the most beautiful cycling trails in the area for those seeking a more difficult trip. The breathtaking vistas of the mountain range make the challenging, winding roads and steep ascent routes worthwhile.

The Greenways of Catalonia, a network of routes that travel through the countryside and along the coast, is yet another fantastic choice for cyclists. These pathways provide you the chance to discover the area's fascinating history as well as its breathtaking natural beauty. You can make pit stops en route to see quaint towns, historic sites, and castles from the Middle Ages.

Whatever bicycle route you decide to take, don't forget to pack plenty of water, sunscreen, and a camera to record all the special moments. Also, keep in mind that cycling is a fascinating and immersive way to see the city and its surroundings in addition to being a fantastic method to exercise.

Golfing

The Real Club de Golf El Prat

The Real Club de Golf El Prat is one of the best places to play golf in Barcelona. This club, which is only 25 minutes from the city center, has 45 holes split over two courses. It's a wonderful spot to challenge your abilities while taking in stunning surroundings, with lovely, lush fairways and difficult bunkers.

The Pitch & Putt Golf Vallromanes

The Pitch & Putt Golf Vallromanes may be something to think about if you're searching for something a little different. The 18-hole course is situated in a gorgeous natural setting with breathtaking vistas of the surrounding hills and valleys. It's a perfect spot to hone your abilities and spend a pleasant day on the course because it was created with both novice and seasoned players in mind.

Adrenaline Pumping Activities

Skydiving:

Visualize descending from an airplane at a speed of more than 200 kph. A once-in-a-lifetime experience like skydiving will make you feel ecstatic and alive. There are a few businesses online that provide skydiving adventures close to Barcelona, with breathtaking views of the surrounding countryside and the Mediterranean Sea.

Bungee jumping:

If you're not quite ready to jump out of an airplane, this might be a better alternative. There are a few bungee jumping spots in Barcelona, one of which is located above a lovely lake. Your heart will undoubtedly race as you plummet toward the water before being pulled back up.

Parasailing:

Have a parasailing excursion to get a bird's eye view of the city and the Mediterranean Sea. You'll be towed behind a speedboat while attached to a parachute and soar over the water. The rush of flying and the excitement of being on the water are both present in this exhilarating experience.

Go-karting:

Visit a go-kart track in Barcelona for a land-based blast of adrenaline. A high-speed race around the track, replete with hairpin curves and tight corners, is what you may challenge your friends or family to. It's a great group activity that's lively and engaging.

Jet skiing:

Feel the wind in your hair as you speed through the waves on a jet ski. A few businesses in Barcelona hire jet skis so that you can tour the shoreline at your own pace. It's a fantastic way to stay cool on a hot day and get an adrenaline boost simultaneously.

Day Trips and Excursions

Girona

A wonderful city with a fascinating history and beautiful architecture, Girona is only one and a half hours north of Barcelona. See the old town's meandering lanes, go across the iconic Eiffel Bridge, and see the magnificent Girona Cathedral.

Girona is truly a remarkable place that transports you back in time with its medieval structures and rich historical buildings. It has a charm that will leave you speechless and captivated.

One of the highlights of Girona is its well-preserved Jewish Quarter, which is a testament to its cultural heritage. The city is also famous for its vibrant annual flower festival, Temps de Flors, where the streets come alive with stunning floral displays. And let's not forget its recent claim to fame as the filming location for Braavos in the popular TV series Game of Thrones.

Located just an hour and a half drive from Barcelona or a convenient 30-minute taxi ride from the airport, Girona is an ideal destination for a day trip or a weekend getaway to escape the hustle and bustle of the city and the overwhelming crowds of tourists.

The best part is that Girona is a walkable city, allowing you to explore all the main attractions on foot. No need to worry about wasting time and money on trains or buses. By strolling through its narrow cobblestone alleyways and admiring the intricate architectural details, you'll truly appreciate the beauty of this city.

Girona Bucket List

- Explore The Cathedral of Santa Maria

When you stroll through Girona, it's impossible to miss the breathtaking Cathedral of Santa Maria. This magnificent structure stands proudly in the city center, towering over everything else. Not only is it the tallest point in Girona, but it also boasts the second largest nave in the world. Prepare to be awestruck by its grandeur and intricate architectural details.

NOTE:

Since the cathedral is a major attraction, it tends to be crowded with tourists taking photos and admiring the building. Want to capture a picture without any tourists in the frame? Visit Girona on a weekday, preferably early in the morning.

Did you feel a sense of déjà vu? Don't worry, you're not going crazy!

The cathedral played a prominent role in season 6 of Game of Thrones, where Girona was transformed into the city of Braavos!

- Indulge in a meal

It's important to keep in mind that many places in Spain (and some across Europe) observe a time of day called siesta. This is when businesses close in the middle of the day, usually around lunchtime, for a few hours of rest before reopening.

While some restaurants remain open during siesta, most follow a specific timeline for serving meals. Lunch is typically served until 3 pm, with dinner starting around 5 or 6 pm (specific times may vary by city). This means that meals may not be available during the siesta period.

Depending on the city and the restaurant, you might find some places offering small appetizers or drinks. In Spain, many restaurants open late and stay open much later than in other countries.

- L'arcaada

Try their artisan panini with arugula salad, followed by their incredible stracciatella ice cream dessert.

- Crepdeque

Head to Crepdeque for the best crepes you'll ever taste. Known for their sweet and savory delights, this small creperie has been a favorite among visitors and locals for years. Just be prepared for long lines—their amazing taste is worth the wait, even in the rain!

- Take a walk along the Carolingian Wall

Considered one of the most Instagram-worthy spots in the city, the Carolingian Wall offers stunning views and historical significance. Girona has faced 25 sieges throughout its history, which explains the high fortifications that still stand today.

The most remarkable of these fortifications is the ancient wall built during the Roman period in the first century BC.

If you venture up to the wall, you'll be walking along the most extensive Carolingian Wall in Europe, and you'll be rewarded with breathtaking views of the entire city.

NOTE:

Climbing up to the wall can be a bit challenging, as there are narrow stairways and uphill tracks. It's not recommended for those who have difficulty walking or climbing inclines.

- Explore Girona's Jewish Quarter

Girona's Jewish Quarter, known as "El Call," is a historic and iconic area in the city. Dating back to the 12th century, it is one of the best-preserved Jewish Quarters in the world.

The quarter is characterized by its narrow streets, beautiful staircases, and various types of arches. At its center, you'll find the Centre Bonastruc ça Porta, the last standing synagogue in Girona. Today, it houses the Jewish History Museum and Institute of Nahmanides Studies.

- Temps De Flors

The best time to visit Girona is during the spectacular flower festival, Temps de Flors. Since its inception in 1954, the festival has transformed the city into a vibrant floral paradise for one week in May. Streets are adorned with magnificent colors and flowers from all over the world.

Every visitor receives a festival map that guides you through each floral installation in the city. Some displays are in plain sight, while others are hidden in secret underground cave tunnels or museums.

Temps de Flors has a magical ability to bring ordinary things to life with beautiful colors and arrangements. It's a sight that shouldn't be missed when visiting Spain. The festival only lasts for a week, but it includes two weekends for everyone to enjoy.

- Enjoy The Quiet Ambiance

Among all the wonderful things that make Girona unique and breathtaking, one of its best features is its tranquil and peaceful ambiance.

While walking along the Rambla de la Libertad, a smaller and quieter version of La Rambla in Barcelona, you'll be surrounded by shops, restaurants, trees, green areas, and courtyards. It seems that despite the annual influx of tourists, the city has also become a popular place for retirees due to its beauty, warm weather, and overall serenity.

- See Eiffel Bridge

The Eiffel Bridge, also known as the Pont de les Peixateries Velles, is an exquisite iron bridge situated in Girona, Spain. It was skillfully designed by Gustave Eiffel, who later went on to create the iconic Eiffel Tower. Positioned at the heart of the city, this bridge is a highly sought-after destination for tourists. Visitors can stroll across the bridge and admire the captivating vistas of Girona and the enchanting Onyar River. Additionally, Girona offers a plethora of other activities to indulge in, including exploring the magnificent Girona Cathedral, immersing in the serene German Gardens or

171

Jardins dels Alemanys, visiting Independence Square, and savoring the finest Gelato in Spain from Rocambolesc.

Tarragona

About one hour south of Barcelona is the coastal city of Tarragona, which is a UNESCO World Heritage site. You can still see the ruins of its old walls, amphitheater, and other remarkable features, which were once part of a significant Roman metropolis. Enjoy the sunshine of the Mediterranean by taking a stroll along the beach.

Tarragona is a city with a rich history spanning over 2200 years, was established by either the Phoenicians or the Iberians and later flourished as a prominent Roman city and port known as Tarraco. It boasts numerous archaeological sites from the Roman era, some of which have been recognized as UNESCO World Heritage Sites. Additionally, Tarragona is home to a cathedral and museums showcasing medieval artifacts.

- Getting To Tarragona

The distance between Barcelona and Tarragona is approximately 82 kilometers (51 miles). If you prefer to drive, the distance by car is around 98.27 km.

When it comes to traveling from Barcelona to Tarragona, there are several transportation options available. One option is to take a train from Barcelona Sants station to Tarragona station. The journey typically takes about 1 hour and the ticket prices range from €7 to €15 depending on the type of train. Another alternative is to take a bus from Barcelona Estació del Nord bus station to Tarragona bus station. The bus ride usually takes about 1 hour and the ticket prices range from €10 to €15.

Tarragona Bucket List

- Check out El Serrallo

First up, you should definitely check out El Serrallo, an old fishing village that's full of character. It's got these vibrant buildings, a bustling port, and a whole bunch of amazing restaurants. Take a leisurely stroll along the seaside promenade or treat yourself to some delicious seafood caught fresh from the local waters.

- Visit El Poblet Monastery

If you're into history, make sure to visit El Poblet Monastery. It's a stunning Gothic complex located just a short drive outside of the city. This place is seriously impressive and it's even recognized as a UNESCO World Heritage Site. Plus, the monastery sits in the middle of the beautiful Catalonian countryside, so you'll get some incredible views of vineyards and mountains.

- Make a stop at the Diocesan Museum

Another must-see in Tarragona is the Diocesan Museum. It's filled with all sorts of fascinating artifacts, like Renaissance tapestries and Roman relics. Seriously, there are over 11,000 works of art here, so it's a dream come true for art and history *lovers.*

Psst...Just a heads up, the museum's opening hours vary depending on the season, so make sure to check their website for the most up-to-date info. And while you're in Tarragona, don't forget to explore the rest of this amazing city with its rich history and archaeological sites. Trust me, you won't be disappointed.

- Check out the Paseo Arqueológico (Murallas)

Now, if you're looking for some outdoor adventure and breathtaking views, I've got just the thing for you. Check out the Paseo Arqueológico (Murallas), a walking path that takes you along the base of the Roman Walls. These walls were built way back in the 3rd to 2nd century BC and they're absolutely mind-blowing. You'll be in awe of how they were constructed without any modern-day tools. As you walk, you'll even come across three intact towers: the Cabiscol Tower, Minerva Tower, and Arzobispo Tower. It's a great way to soak up the city's two-thousand-year history.

- Enjoy spectacular views from Ferreres Aqueduct

And if you're in need of some fresh air and a break from the crowds, head over to the Ferreres Aqueduct. This ancient bridge, also known as Pont de les Ferreres or Pont del Diable, is located just 4km north of the city center. It was originally built to supply water to the people of Tarraco. With its 36 arches and towering height, it's a sight to behold. You can even walk along the bridge for a different perspective of the area. Don't worry, it's perfectly safe!

To get to the Ferreres Aqueduct, you can catch bus #5 from Tarragona's main square towards San Salvador. Just hop off after 5 minutes at the Pont del Diable. If you have a vehicle, you can take the N-240 towards Lleida. You'll definitely want to add this unique experience to your Tarragona itinerary and get a taste of the city's rich history.

- Visit the Tarragona Cathedral

Make sure to visit the Tarragona Cathedral, a stunning structure with a diverse history. It offers multimedia video guides for a more immersive experience. Admission fees and opening times can be found on their website. I recommend visiting early in the morning to avoid crowds.

Tarragona Cathedral

- See the Roman Forum

The Roman Forum is a must-see for history enthusiasts. As a UNESCO Site, it showcases ancient ruins that provide insight into local life in ancient Tarraco.

- Relax at the Beaches

Take some time to relax at the beautiful beaches in Tarragona. Playa El Miracle is a popular choice, but there are many other options to explore along the Costa Dorada.

- Stroll through Rambla Nova

Stroll through Rambla Nova, a vibrant street filled with shops, restaurants, and balconies adorned with plants. Don't forget to visit Balcon de Mediterráneo for a breathtaking view of the city and ocean. Check out the Als Castellers Monument, a life-size structure representing the Catalonian tradition of human towers.

- Enjoy the City center and the murals

Finally, immerse yourself in the colorful city center, where you'll find unique boutiques, art galleries, and charming squares. Take a moment to sit on a terraza and soak up the atmosphere. Look out for Plaça dels Sedassos to see a beautiful mural depicting Spanish balconies and its citizens. Enjoy your time in Tarragona.

Sitges

Sitges gained fame in the late 19th century as a trendy and artistic hub, drawing in writers, artists, and thinkers who were captivated by its charm. Back then, it was just a quaint fishing village, but it captured the hearts and ignited the creativity of these intellectuals. Sitges' artistic reputation traces its origins to that time when painter Santiago Rusiñol made it his summer retreat. Fast forward to the 1960s, during the Francoist regime in mainland Spain, and Sitges transformed into a haven for the counterculture movement. It earned the nickname "Ibiza in miniature," becoming a vibrant center for those seeking a taste of rebellion and alternative lifestyle.

Getting to Sitges

If you're planning a trip from Barcelona to Sitges, you've got a few options to choose from. One way to go is by hopping on the train at Estación de tren Barcelona-Passeig De Gracia and heading to Estación de tren Sitges. It's a quick journey, taking around 44 minutes, and the ticket prices range from €5 to €8. Another option is catching a bus from Barcelona to Sitges - Parc Can Robert. The bus ride usually takes about 55 minutes, and the fare falls between €4 and €7. And of course, if you prefer the freedom of driving, it's about a 45-minute trip without any traffic or hold-ups. Just get on the B-10 Highway, head south, then continue onto the C-32 and take Exit 30.

Sitges Bucket List

- Explore Cau Ferrat Museum

Make sure to check out the Cau Ferrat Museum when you're in Sitges. It was established back in 1893 by the artist Santiago

177

Rusiñol, and it's definitely a must-see. Inside, you'll discover an impressive collection of various art forms that Rusiñol gathered throughout his life. From stunning wrought iron pieces to ceramics, glasswork, and even modern paintings, drawings, and sculptures. The museum houses works by renowned artists like Picasso, Catalan and French artists, as well as pieces by anonymous creators. While exploring the museum, you'll learn that it got its name, Cau Ferrat, because it used to be a meeting spot for artists (Cau means "nest" in Catalan), and Ferrat refers to the iron that Rusiñol was particularly fond of collecting.

- Visit Museu de Maricel

Another museum worth visiting is the Museu de Maricel. Here, you'll find artworks spanning from the 10th century to the first half of the 20th century, showcasing a range of styles from realism to other artistic movements. The museum features collections from Dr. Jesus Perez-Rosales and the Villa de Sitges. If you're interested, they also offer guided tours to enhance your experience.

- Visit Museu Romantic

Don't forget to pay a visit to the Museu Romantic during your time in Sitges. This unique museum is situated in a beautiful late 18th-century house and provides a fascinating glimpse into the lifestyle of a well-to-do Catalan family during the Romantic era. Step back in time as you explore the museum and get a vivid re-creation of the daily life of a Sitges land-owning family from the 18th and 19th centuries.

What makes the Museu Romantic particularly intriguing are the family rooms filled with exquisite furniture and household objects. You'll be captivated by the carefully curated displays that showcase the tastes, preferences, and opulent living conditions of that era. It's an immersive experience that allows you to envision the world of an affluent Catalan family during the Romantic movement. Make sure to take your time and soak in the interesting details and stories that unfold throughout the museum.

- Visit the Stämpfli Foundation

You should definitely make a stop at the Stämpfli Foundation during your visit. It's home to one of the most significant contemporary art collections in Catalonia. Pere and Anna Maria Stampfli, a couple who are passionate about art, have played a key role in promoting this foundation. The collection, which consists of 60 works by 90 artists from 22 different countries, is on display at the foundation's premises in Placa de l'Ajuntament de Sitges.

What makes this collection truly special is that all the artworks have been generously donated by the artists themselves, their descendants, or renowned gallery owners. Together, these pieces form a remarkable body of contemporary art that spans the last 50 years. It's a unique opportunity to immerse yourself in the vibrant and diverse world of contemporary art, all under one roof.

- The beaches

Make sure to explore stunning beaches. They're the city's main tourist attraction. The beaches are divided into three sections: Levante, central, and western beaches, each catering to different preferences. If the weather is pleasant and you're up for a leisurely stroll, you can easily walk to all of them.

- Sant Sebastia beach

One beach worth visiting is Sant Sebastia beach. It's an urban beach that's perfect for families, stretching about 200 meters long and 20 meters wide. You'll find essential amenities such as lifeguards, a beach bar, umbrellas, and hammocks. It's also wheelchair accessible with a convenient ramp. Located behind the San Bartolomé church, this beach serves as a gateway to the historic center of Sitges.

- Walk along the promenade

For a delightful experience, take a leisurely walk along the Sitges Seafront Promenade. This scenic route stretches about 2.5 kilometers and offers stunning views of the sea. You can choose to walk, rent a bicycle, or even try a segway for added fun. The path is flat and straightforward, running parallel to the coastline. Along the way, you can take breaks, rest, or even take a refreshing dip at any of the beautiful beaches you encounter. Starting from Fragata beach, where the Bartolomé church is located, you can complete the tour at the Terramar gardens.

To return, you can either retrace your steps along the same path or wander through the charming streets of the residential neighborhood of Terramar and Vinyet. It's a fantastic way to explore the surroundings and enjoy the scenic beauty of Sitges.

- Visit to the House of Bacardi

Make sure to add a visit to the House of Bacardi to your itinerary when you're in Sitges. Did you know that the famous Bacardi family is originally from Sitges? That's right, the ones behind the renowned rum! The Casa Bacardi tour is a must-do experience while in Sitges. You'll get to learn about the fascinating story of Facundo Bacardi, who was born in Sitges and later emigrated to Cuba in the mid-19th century. He founded Casa Bacardi in Cuba, and his family continues to run the business he established back in 1862. During the tour, you'll discover the process of how Bacardi rum is crafted and even get to taste some of the ingredients. To top it off, they offer a cocktail lesson where you'll learn how to make four different cocktails. Afterward, you can relax on the terrace, sipping your own handcrafted cocktail on one of the comfy sofas.

- Vilarnau Wineries

Another great visit is the Vilarnau Wineries. They offer an exciting guided tour where you can explore the vineyards on a segway. Don't worry if you've never ridden one before; they'll teach you how. During the tour, you'll get a close-up look at the vines and grapes. Alternatively, you can opt for a walking tour where you'll learn the essential concepts and then delve into the cellars to discover the wine-making process. Ever wondered what sets cava apart from sparkling wine or everyday wine? You'll learn all about it during this visit. And, of course, it wouldn't be complete without a tasting session where they teach you how to appreciate the different qualities of cava.

- Calle del Pecado

For some leisurely shopping and dining, take a stroll down Calle del Pecado, also known as Sin Street. It's Sitges' bustling downtown area, filled with a mix of restaurants, bars, clothing stores, and souvenir shops. This vibrant street, officially known as Calle 1 de Mayo, is renowned as the city's best-known bar area. It's the perfect place to enjoy a night out, whether you want to dance the night away or simply relax with a refreshing drink in hand.

- Attend a festival

Make sure not to miss the major festival of Santa Tecla when you're in Sitges. This festival honors San Bartolomé and Santa Tecla, who have been the patron saints of Sitges since the late 16th century. Previously, only Santa Tecla held this distinction. The festival is a lively celebration where the entire town gets involved. While it may be quieter compared to other festivals in Sitges, it's definitely worth experiencing.

During the Santa Tecla festival, you'll notice the city's balconies adorned with decorations, including white flags featuring the red cross of Sant Jordi and the coat of arms of Sitges. Participants dress in white attire, complemented by red scarves, helmets, colorful hats, and espadrilles adorned with blue and red ribbons. This Traditional Festival of National Interest has been celebrated since 1991.

The festivities in Sitges typically take place in August and September. On August 24, the Festa Major de Sitges honors Sant Bartomeu, while on September 23, the festival celebrates Santa Tecla. As the dates are close to each other, the two festivities are often unified and celebrated between mid and late August. The Santa Tecla festival is a vibrant event filled with traditions, rituals, colorful displays, and mesmerizing fireworks, particularly the "Diables de Sitges" performance.

- Pay a visit to the Church of Sant Bartomeu and Santa Tecla

While in Sitges, don't miss the opportunity to visit the Church of Sant Bartomeu and Santa Tecla. This iconic church, featured in many postcards of the city, was built in the 17th century and underwent several modifications over time. It boasts a Baroque style and is situated in the same location where two previous churches stood, one Romanesque and the other Gothic, dating back to 1322. Inside the church, you can admire various altarpieces, including the central Renaissance-style one depicting San Bartolomé and Santa Tecla, the Renaissance Roser altarpiece, and two Baroque altarpieces. The church's organ also showcases a Baroque style.

- Explore Palau Maricel

Another notable building in Sitges is the Palau Maricel, also known as Maricel de Terra to distinguish it from the Museu Maricel mentioned earlier. The Palau features several remarkable spaces, such as the Salo d'Or, the Blue Room, the Chapel Room, the Vaixells Room, the Terraces, and the Cloister,

183

offering breathtaking views of the Mediterranean. This modernist palace displays unique decorations and serves as a venue for institutional and cultural events, including concerts, conferences, and presentations. It is also rented for company events and weddings. In the summer, you can visit the rooms, terrace, and cloister organized by Museus de Sitges.

- Find tranquility at the Raco of Calm

For a peaceful retreat, head to the Raco of Calm, a beloved spot among locals due to its tranquility and proximity to the sea. This serene corner is an ideal location for concerts, thanks to its excellent acoustics. It's situated in the old town of Sitges, on a narrow street that connects the Palau Maricel and the Cau Ferrat Museum with the parish church of San Bartolomé and Santa Tecla.

Costa Brava

The Costa Brava is a stunning coastline that is close to Barcelona and is renowned for its rocky cliffs, secret bays, and blue waters. Explore the coast on a boat excursion, or go hiking to find some of the area's best-kept secrets.

If you're looking for a breathtaking coastal experience in northeastern Spain, Costa Brava is the place to be. This stunning region encompasses the counties of Alt Empordà, Baix Empordà, and Selva in the province of Girona. What sets Costa Brava apart is its rugged coastline, adorned with picturesque coves and beautiful beaches. In fact, the name

Costa Brava translates to "rugged coast" in Catalan. The region boasts a fascinating history that dates back to the time of the Roman Empire and has been influenced by various cultures throughout the centuries.

Getting to Costa Brava

To reach Costa Brava from Barcelona, you have a couple of transportation options. You can hop on a train or take a bus. The train journey typically takes around 1 hour and 30 minutes, departing from Barcelona Sants station and arriving at Girona station. Once you reach Girona, you can easily reach your desired destination in Costa Brava by taking a bus or a taxi. On the other hand, if you opt for the bus, the travel time is approximately 2 hours and 30 minutes. The bus departs from Barcelona Nord station and arrives at Girona bus station. Whichever mode of transportation you choose, get ready to embark on an unforgettable adventure along the stunning Costa Brava coastline.

Costa Brava Bucket List

Costa Brava offers a plethora of activities for tourists to enjoy. One of the highlights is exploring the stunning coastline, with its rugged beauty and numerous small coves and beaches. You can spend your time soaking up the sun, taking refreshing dips in the crystal-clear waters, and building sandcastles to your heart's content. If you're an adventure enthusiast, there are plenty of water-based activities to try out, such as kayaking, kitesurfing, water-skiing, and even going on exhilarating cruises or sailing trips.

A visit to the charming city of Girona is a must-do, especially for those who appreciate medieval architecture. You'll be captivated by the well-preserved buildings and fascinating history that surrounds you as you wander through its narrow streets. And don't miss the opportunity to visit the Salvador Dalí Theatre-Museum, where you can delve into the imaginative and surreal world of the renowned artist.

- Take a wine tour

If you have a taste for wine, consider going on a wine tour in Costa Brava. You'll have the chance to explore local vineyards, learn about the winemaking process, and, of course, savor some exquisite wines. For those who prefer a more leisurely pastime, golfing is available in picturesque settings, providing a relaxing and enjoyable experience.

- Explore the beaches

Embark on an exploration of the stunning beaches along the Costa Brava. Whether you prefer the hidden inlets of Calella de Palafrugell or the tranquil coves of Blanes, there's a stretch of golden sand for everyone. If sunbathing isn't your thing, take a stroll along the coastal paths that offer breathtaking views. For more details on the best beaches in Costa Brava, check out our blog!

- Enjoy the Landscape

Prepare to be amazed by the captivating landscape of Costa Brava. With its sweeping bays, dramatic cliffs, protected marshes, and sand dunes, the coastal scenery is a sight to behold. Venture inland and you'll encounter picturesque white-washed villages adorned with vibrant bougainvillea. Don't forget to admire the lush foothills of the Pyrenees that inspired the renowned artist Salvador Dali.

- Go swimming

Families will find plenty to enjoy in Costa Brava. The city of Girona is a vibrant destination with bustling markets and lively street performers. Many pristine Blue Flag beaches in the area are perfect for children. You'll also find resorts that have been awarded the Family Tourist Destination seal, ensuring a fantastic experience for the whole family.

- Learn about Costa Brava history

Costa Brava is steeped in history and culture, tracing back to ancient times. Explore the Roman, Medieval, and Arab influences seen in Gothic buildings, hilltop castles, and ancient monuments. The walled city of Girona is particularly noteworthy, offering historic treasures and panoramic views. Immerse yourself in the rich heritage of the region.

- Attend a festival

Join in the vibrant festivals that the Catalans are famous for. Plan your Costa Brava holiday around one of Catalonia's outstanding celebrations. Experience the lively carnivals in February or witness the spectacular Fireworks Contest in Blanes during July. The Porta Ferrada music festival and

Girona Flower Festival are also popular events that attract crowds.

- Visit Mas Molla Winery

Indulge in a visit to the esteemed Mas Molla winery. This family-run establishment offers insights into traditional farming methods that have been passed down through generations. Discover the excellence of Costa Brava's wineries, which are highly regarded throughout Spain.

- Explore Gala Dali's Castle

For art enthusiasts, a visit to Gala Dali's castle is a must. Explore the Dali Theatre Museum in Girona and the Salvador Dali house in Port Lligat, Cadaqués. Take the opportunity to visit the "Gala Dali Castle," which serves as the former home and now the mausoleum of the legendary painter's wife.

- Visit Begur

Follow in the footsteps of the locals and make a stop at the charming town of Begur. Its colorful historic quarter and 15th-century hilltop castle make it one of the most beautiful towns in Costa Brava. Immerse yourself in its charm and beauty.

Additionally, history enthusiasts will find megalithic complexes waiting to be explored, offering insights into the region's ancient past. And of course, no visit to Costa Brava would be complete without indulging in the local gastronomy. From fresh seafood delicacies to mouthwatering traditional dishes, there's a wide array of culinary delights to satisfy your taste buds. So be sure to immerse yourself in the vibrant flavors of the region and discover the gastronomic treasures that Costa Brava has to offer.

Vilafranca del Penedès

Cheers, wine lovers! Only one hour from Barcelona, the stunning wine area of Penedès is renowned for making some of the world's best sparkling wines. See the vineyards, discover how wine is made, and savor some of the mouthwatering regional wines.

Penedès, a wine region, is a great place to visit if you're in Barcelona. It's only about 37 kilometers (23 miles) away, or roughly a 48.8-kilometer (30.3-mile) drive.

- Getting There:

Train: The Renfe R4 train line is your best bet. It runs from Barcelona Sants station to Vilafranca del Penedès, the capital of the region. It's a quick 30-minute journey.

Bus: If you prefer buses, there are several companies that operate between Barcelona and Penedès. The bus ride typically takes around 50 minutes.

Car: Driving is also an option. It'll take you approximately 40 minutes to reach Penedès from Barcelona.

The choice of transportation depends on your budget and how much time you have. If you're watching your wallet, the bus is the most affordable option. But if you're short on time and want to get there quickly, the train is the fastest. And if you want the freedom to explore the region at your own pace, driving is your best bet.

Here's a quick summary of the travel options:

Train: 30 minutes, costs between €4-€8.

Bus: 50 minutes, costs between €4-€8.

Car: 40 minutes, costs between €5-€10.

Penedès Bucket List

- Torres

Let me tell you about the biggest winery in Spain, which has a fascinating history. It was established way back in 1870 and has been crafting exceptional cava and wines for more than 140 years. Their dedication to quality has made them renowned worldwide. Not only do they have an impressive array of vineyards in Penedès, but they've also expanded their operations to Chile and other important wine regions in Spain.

- Visit Freixenet

Let's take a trip back to 1911 when Freixenet, a legendary winery in Penedès, emerged on the scene. This family-run business has been a major player ever since, dedicated to crafting the most exquisite sparkling wine you can imagine. And boy, did they succeed!

Their creation caught the attention of wine enthusiasts not just in Spain but across the globe, propelling them to become the top producer of sparkling wine in the 1980s.

Fast forward to today, and Freixenet is all about embracing cutting-edge technology and innovative approaches. They've revolutionized the Spanish cava industry with their tech-savvy mindset. From utilizing new grape pressing techniques to even incorporating space technology into their processes, this family has truly changed the game.

While you're sipping on a glass of Freixenet, remember and appreciate the rich history and trailblazing spirit behind the brand. They've come a long way since 1911, and their commitment to pushing boundaries and delivering exceptional sparkling wine continues to shape the industry.

- Cava Rimarts

You absolutely must try the wines from Cava Rimarts. They are known for their exceptional artisanal wines and cavas. What sets them apart is their deep appreciation for Mother Nature and their commitment to using natural, traditional methods. Even though they're relatively new to the winery scene in Penedès, having been founded in 1987, they have quickly made a name for themselves. Their unwavering philosophy and innovative approach have allowed them to stand shoulder to shoulder with the more established bodegas in the region.

Figueres

Salvador Dal's birthplace, Figueres, is a must-visit destination for art fans. See the town's numerous art galleries, take in the

191

enchanting medieval architecture, and pay a visit to the Dali Theatre Museum.

Figueres has an incredibly interesting history. It all started way back in Roman times when it was just a small settlement. Since then, it has seen the rise and fall of different civilizations like the Visigoths and Moors.

During the Middle Ages, Figueres became a fortified town and played a crucial role in defending Catalonia against invasions. It was a bustling hub for trade and became quite prosperous under the rule of the Counts of Empúries and later the Kings of Aragon.

In the 18th century, things took a bit of a downturn for Figueres due to wars and conflicts, but fear not, because the city bounced back in the 19th century with the Industrial Revolution. Textile manufacturing and trade took off, leading to economic growth and urban development.

Now, here's where it gets really exciting. Figueres is forever tied to the legendary surrealist artist, Salvador Dalí. He was actually born in Figueres in 1904, and his influence is everywhere. The mind-blowing Dalí Theatre-Museum stands as a testament to his artistry and imagination.

Fun fact: Dalí is even buried there!

Today, Figueres has become a vibrant cultural and tourist hotspot. It retains its historical charm while embracing modern developments. Plus, its proximity to the stunning Costa Brava coastline adds to its allure.

Figueres Bucket List

- ## La Rambla in Figueres

Take a leisurely stroll down La Rambla in Figueres, unlike its bustling counterpart in Barcelona. This version of La Rambla offers a serene and calming atmosphere. With plenty of benches and towering trees, it's the perfect spot to people-watch, unwind, and escape the scorching summer sun. During our visit, we took a break for some coffee, enjoying the art of observing people while reminiscing about our mind-blowing experience at the Dali Museum.

- ## Salvador Dali House

Make sure to visit the birth house of Salvador Dali.. You'll find pictures of Dali's family displayed outside the house, but unfortunately, you can't go inside the building itself.

- ## Església de Sant Pere

Don't forget to make a quick visit to the Església de Sant Pere church while you're on your way to La Rambla. It's conveniently located near the Salvador Dali Theater Museum. The church welcomes tourists during the day, and the best part is, there's no entrance fee. Take your time to explore the interior of the church and be captivated by the beauty of its stained glass windows. Keep an eye out for the mesmerizing rose window, especially when the sun is shining—it's a sight to behold

Chapter Seven

Practical Matters

Accommodations

Barcelona is a dynamic and engaging city that provides a variety of lodging choices to accommodate all types of travelers. The city offers a wide range of lodging options, including opulent hotels, quaint bed & breakfasts, and inexpensive hostels. Let's examine some of the greatest places to stay in Barcelona, highlighting their merits so you can pick the one that best satisfies your requirements.

Luxury Hotels

Many upscale hotels in Barcelona provide first-rate amenities and services for people looking for luxury. A prime example of this is the **Mandarin Oriental**, which is situated in the center of the city. The hotel has a lavish spa, a Michelin-starred restaurant, and a beautiful rooftop terrace with panoramic city views. **Hotel Sixtytwo Barcelona, The One Barcelona** and **Ohla Barcelona** are also great options.

Boutique Accommodations

Consider booking a room at one of Barcelona's beautiful bed and breakfasts if you're seeking a more distinctive experience.

The Gothic Quarter's Petit Palace Boqueria Garden is the ideal option. This charming boutique hotel has a tranquil garden terrace, up-to-date, chic accommodations, and a perfect location next to the well-known La Boqueria market. Check out **Casa Bonay** and **The Barcelona Edition** too.

Budget

Barcelona also has a wide selection of inexpensive hostels for those on a tight budget. A nice choice is the chic Gracia neighborhood's **Generator Hostel**. This hostel is ideal for young visitors wishing to meet new people and enjoy the city on a budget because it has a fun environment, cozy dorms, and private rooms. Check out **St Christopher Inn/Hostel** and **Safestay Barcelona Passieg de Gracia; they** have a free wifi feature. **TOC Hostel Barcelona** offers free pool facilities.

Vacation Rentals

Seeking a distinctive experience? You may live like a local and fully immerse yourself in the city's culture by choosing from a variety of apartments and homes available on Airbnb in Barcelona. There are accommodations for every taste and price range, ranging from small apartments to roomy lofts.

Vaccinations:

Barcelona does not require any vaccines for entry.

The World Health Organization does, however, advise routine immunizations against diseases like polio, hepatitis B, measles, mumps, rubella, diphtheria, tetanus, pertussis, and rubella.

Visa Prerequisites

- Barcelona does not require a visa for citizens of the European Union (EU) or the European Economic Area (EEA).
- For up to 90 days, nationals of a select group of nations—including the United States, Canada, Australia, and Japan—may enter Barcelona without a visa.
- Barcelona may require a visa for visitors from foreign nations. To find out the prerequisites, it is advised to contact the Spanish Embassy or Consulate in your nation.

Paper specifications

- All tourists are required to have a passport that is current and has at least three months left on it after their intended stay in Barcelona.
- A return ticket, evidence of sufficient finances, or extra papers, such as proof of further travel, may be needed by some nations.

It is crucial to remember that these criteria could change, therefore it is advised to check with the relevant authorities before traveling to make sure you have the right paperwork and immunizations.

Avoiding Long Queues:

- Consider purchasing skip-the-line tickets for popular attractions to avoid long queues.
- Visit popular attractions during off-peak hours to avoid crowds and long queues.
- Use public transportation, such as buses and trains, to avoid traffic and long queues at toll booths.
- Book watersport equipment rentals and in advance for the best deals.
- Use popular sites like booking.com and TripAdvisor and always compare the prices before making any decisions.

General Travel Advice:

Research the culture and customs of Barcelona before traveling to ensure you are respectful and aware of local norms

Purchase travel insurance to protect yourself against unexpected events, such as illness or theft

Always carry identification and emergency contact information with you

Stay aware of your surroundings and avoid areas that may be unsafe or have a high crime rate.

Money and Tipping

The euro is the official currency of Barcelona. It is advised to exchange money at banks or exchange offices because these locations frequently provide better exchange rates than accommodations or airports.

Credit cards: In Barcelona, especially in tourist districts, credit cards are readily accepted. The most widely used credit cards are Visa and Mastercard, followed by American Express and Diners Club. For smaller transactions or if you travel somewhere that doesn't accept credit cards, it's always a good idea to have some cash on hand.

Tipping: Although it is not customary, tipping is appreciated in Barcelona. In restaurants, a service charge is frequently already added to the bill, but if you thought the service was particularly good, you can increase it by 5 to 10%. Taxi drivers do not expect tips, but it is customary to round up to the nearest Euro.

ATMs: There are many ATMs in Barcelona, and the majority of them accept foreign bank cards. However, be warned that your home bank can charge you an ATM fee if you use an ATM abroad.

Budgeting: Barcelona is often a cheap city for tourists, although prices might change depending on the time of year and where you are. While lodging in the city center is typically more expensive, staying in the suburbs can be more

198

cost-effective. Moreover, food and beverages can cost more in tourist regions than in local restaurants. But if you go about and explore the city, you can discover plenty of great and reasonably priced options.

Safety and emergency contacts

- Pickpocketing is a typical occurrence in tourist destinations, particularly in congested areas like Las Ramblas, the metro, and buses. Keep your possessions close at hand and refrain from carrying a lot of cash or valuables in your pockets.

- Remain in crowded, well-lit areas at night: If you're out at night, try to stay away from secluded or gloomy regions.

- Be on the lookout for scams: sadly, some con artists target tourists in Barcelona. Be wary of persons who try to divert you or offer you "free" stuff so that someone else can steal your belongings.

- For police, fire, or medical assistance in an emergency, phone 112, the European emergency number. You can dial 092 if you require police assistance but it is not an emergency.

- The Catalan police force, the Mossos d'Esquadra, has a specific unit for tourist aid that can assist you in a variety of languages if you require assistance or information. They are located at 17-S Plaça Catalunya.

- You can get maps at hotels, the airport or bookstores. Always keep one handy or use Google maps.

Medical Assistance

You can go to a hospital or clinic if you require medical assistance. **Hospital Clinic de Barcelona** and **Hospital del Mar** are a few of Barcelona's top medical facilities.

Internet and Telecommunications

SIM cards: Spain's major mobile network operators, such as Orange, Vodafone, or Movistar, offers tourists the opportunity to acquire a local SIM card. Official retailers, supermarkets, and a few convenience stores sell these SIM cards. Visitors must provide their passports to register their SIM cards, which normally cost between €5 and €15.

Wi-Fi hotspots: Barcelona has a lot of free public Wi-Fi hotspots for visitors to use. The most well-liked locations with free Wi-Fi include public parks, museums, and coffee shops. Use public WiFi with caution, though, as it's not always reliable and secure.

Visitors can rent portable Wi-Fi equipment—also referred to as pocket Wi-Fi—from some Barcelona-based service providers. For a daily or weekly rental price, these gadgets enable guests to access the internet from anywhere in the city.

Data roaming is another option open to travelers through their home mobile network provider. To avoid any unexpected costs while traveling, it is advised to ask your operator about their international roaming rates before leaving. Data roaming, however, can be pricey.

Internet cafes: Barcelona is home to a large number of internet cafes that provide access to the internet for a little cost.

Final Overview of Barcelona's Boroughs

Barcelona is divided into ten districts, or boroughs, known as "distritos" in Spanish and "districtes" in Catalan. These districts are further divided into smaller neighborhoods or "barrios." The ten districts of Barcelona are:

Ciutat Vella (Old City):

This district encompasses the historic center of Barcelona
This historic district is divided into four main areas that each offer their own unique charm: El Raval, Barri Gòtic (Gothic Quarter), La Ribera/El Born, and Barceloneta. Get ready to immerse yourself in the captivating atmosphere and discover the must-see attractions within the old city!

- **Barri Gòtic** (Gothic Quarter): Step into the oldest and most atmospheric part of Barcelona. Picture narrow alleyways, hidden plazas, and a treasure trove of historic buildings. It's a delightful labyrinth where you can wander and uncover the rich history and architectural gems that bring the past to life.

- **La Rambla:** Get ready to stroll along the iconic pedestrian street that cuts through the heart of the old town. La Rambla is a bustling thoroughfare where you'll find a mix of shops, street performers, cafes, and vibrant energy. It's the perfect spot for people-watching and immersing yourself in the lively ambiance.

- **La Catedral:** Prepare to be in awe of the stunning Gothic cathedral located in the heart of the Gothic Quarter. Its grandeur and intricate details are a sight to behold. Take a moment to step inside, admire the magnificent interior, and soak up the spiritual atmosphere.

- **Palau de la Música Catalana**: Music enthusiasts, this one's for you! This concert hall is a masterpiece of Catalan modernista architecture, designed by the talented architect Lluís Domènech i Montaner. Its exquisite design and intricate stained glass create a magical setting for unforgettable musical performances.

- **Mercat de la Boqueria**: Indulge your senses in this vibrant public market. Explore the lively stalls, where you'll find a wide array of fresh produce, tantalizing meats, delectable seafood, and an abundance of other culinary delights. It's a food lover's paradise.

- **Basílica de Santa Maria del Mar**: Discover the beauty of this Gothic church nestled in the La Ribera/El Born neighborhood. Its soaring architecture and serene ambiance make it a true gem. Take a moment to appreciate the intricate details and the centuries of history that this church holds.

- **Palau Güell**: Marvel at the architectural brilliance of Antoni Gaudí at this stunning mansion. The Palau Güell was designed by Gaudí for his patron Eusebi Güell, and it showcases the unique and visionary style that Gaudí is renowned for. It's a testament to the city's artistic legacy.

- **Parc de la Ciutadella**: Escape the hustle and bustle of the city in this expansive park. Explore its lush landscapes, visit the zoo, admire the serene lake, and even discover several museums within the park. Don't miss the striking Catalan Parliament building that adds a touch of grandeur to the surroundings.

Eixample

The Eixample district is one of the most iconic and distinctive areas of Barcelona. Designed in the 19th century by urban planner Ildefons Cerdà, it is characterized by its grid-like layout, wide streets, and renowned modernist architecture. Eixample is divided into two main sections: Eixample Esquerra (Left Eixample) and Eixample Dreta (Right Eixample), with the famous Passeig de Gràcia serving as a central axis.

Eixample is known for its architectural masterpieces, including the world-famous Sagrada Família, designed by Antoni Gaudí

The top places to see in Eixample are:

- Sagrada Família
- Casa Batlló
- Casa Milà (La Pedrera)
- Passeig de Gràcia

Hidden Gems in Eixample:

Eixample is like a treasure trove, hiding away unique experiences and delightful surprises. Let me share some of the hidden gems you can discover in this vibrant district of Barcelona:

- **Casa de les Punxes**: Designed by Josep Puig i Cadafalch, this modernist building is a hidden gem with its medieval-inspired towers and a facade that catches your eye. Take a guided tour to explore its intriguing interior and unravel its fascinating history.

- **Sant Pau Recinte Modernista**: Often overshadowed by its famous neighbor, the Hospital de Sant Pau, this modernist complex is a true hidden treasure. Immerse yourself in its enchanting architecture, intricate mosaics, and serene gardens.

- **Mercat de la Concepció**: Nestled within the streets of Eixample, this local market is a lively and atmospheric gem. Stroll through its stalls brimming with fresh produce, local delicacies, and vibrant flowers, and soak up the authentic market ambiance.

- **Palau Baró de Quadras:** A hidden gem tucked away on Avinguda Diagonal, this modernist palace is often overlooked. Its awe-inspiring facade and home to the Institut Ramon Llull, promoting Catalan culture and language, make it a worthwhile discovery.

- **El Nacional**: Prepare to be surprised by this hidden gastronomic gem housed in a beautifully restored building. Step inside and be delighted by the diverse culinary offerings, with dedicated sections for various cuisines, all within a stylish setting.

Sants-Montjuïc

This cool district is situated in the southeast part of the city and has some pretty awesome stuff to check out. One of the main attractions is the Parc de Montjuïc, which is like a whole world of its own. You've got museums, a legit castle, and the most amazing views of the city. Seriously, it's a must-visit. And if you're wondering what else you can do there, well, let me give you the lowdown on some of the top attractions you'll find in Sants-Montjuïc.

Top Attractions

- **Montjuïc Hill:** This iconic hill provides panoramic views of Barcelona and is home to several key attractions, including: Montjuïc Castle (Castell de Montjuïc): Magic Fountain of Montjuïc and the Montjuïc Olympic Stadium (Estadi Olímpic Lluís Companys).

- One of the most exciting ways to get to the top of the city is by taking a ride on the **Montjuïc cable car**. It's not only a convenient mode of transportation, but it also offers breathtaking views that will leave you in awe. Once you reach the top, you'll find yourself at the magnificent Montjuïc Castle. From here, you can enjoy panoramic views of Barcelona that are simply stunning. It's the perfect spot to take some incredible photos and soak in the beauty of the city.

- Another must-visit attraction in Sants-Montjuïc is the **Palau Nacional**. This majestic palace was originally built for the 1929 International Exhibition and now houses the National Art Museum of Catalonia. It's a treasure trove of art and culture, showcasing a wide range of works that will captivate any art lover.

- If you're interested in Spanish architecture, make sure to visit **Poble Espanyol**. This open-air museum is a replica of a Spanish village and features stunning architecture from all over Spain.

- Art enthusiasts shouldn't miss out on La **Fundació Miró**, a museum dedicated to the works of Joan Miró.

- For nature lovers, **El Jardin Botanico** is a must-visit. This botanical garden is home to over 2000 species of plants from around the world. It's a peaceful oasis where you can escape the hustle and bustle of the city and reconnect with nature.

- One of the most iconic attractions in Sants-Montjuïc is the **Font Mágica**, or Magic Fountain. Located at the base of Montjuïc hill, this fountain puts on a mesmerizing light and music show that will leave you spellbound. It's a truly magical experience that shouldn't be missed.

- If you're looking for a place to relax and unwind, the **Montjuïc Cemetery** is the perfect spot. Known for its beautiful sculptures and serene atmosphere, it offers a peaceful place for reflection and contemplation.

- Sports enthusiasts will be thrilled to visit the **Montjuïc Olympic Stadium**, which was the main venue for the 1992 Summer Olympics. Today, it serves as a sports and entertainment venue, hosting various events throughout the year.

- And finally, don't forget to visit the **Montjuïc Communications Tower**. Designed by the renowned architect Santiago Calatrava, this striking tower offers panoramic views of Barcelona and is an architectural marvel in itself.

Hidden Gems in Sants-Montjuïc

- Explore the **Jardins de Mossèn Costa i Llobera**, a tucked-away garden on Montjuïc Hill. It's a paradise for succulent and cacti enthusiasts, with an incredible variety of plants to admire as you wander through the peaceful paths.

- Experience the vintage charm of **El Molino**, an iconic theater and cabaret venue. It's a hidden gem where you can catch live music, comedy, and flamenco performances, transporting you back to another era.

- Unwind in the lesser-known **Parc de l'Escorxador**, a tranquil park near the Sants neighborhood. Whether you want to relax, have a picnic, or watch locals skate in the dedicated park, this hidden oasis is the perfect spot to escape the hustle and bustle.

Les Corts

A residential district that houses the Camp Nou stadium, home to FC Barcelona.

Les Corts might not be as famous among tourists as other areas, but it still has its fair share of attractions to offer. Here are some of the top sights you should check out when you're in Les Corts:

Camp Nou: If you're a football fan or simply curious about the sport, you can't miss a visit to Camp Nou, the iconic home stadium of FC Barcelona. Take a tour, visit the museum, and immerse yourself in the rich history and passion of the club.

Pedralbes Monastery: Step back in time at the enchanting Pedralbes Monastery, a centuries-old Gothic-style monastery. Explore the peaceful courtyard, visit the church, and discover the monastery's fascinating past through its museum.

L'Illa Diagonal: If shopping and dining are on your agenda, head to L'Illa Diagonal, a large shopping center offering a wide range of stores, boutiques, and eateries. It's the perfect place to indulge in some retail therapy or enjoy a delicious meal.

Plaça de la Concòrdia: This delightful square in Les Corts invites you to take a break and savor the moment. With charming buildings and cozy outdoor cafes, it's a lovely spot to sit back, relax, and soak up the local vibe.

Palau Reial de Pedralbes: Explore the majestic Palau Reial de Pedralbes, once a royal residence. Its stunning architecture and lush gardens provide a serene backdrop for a leisurely stroll or a visit to its museum.

Parc de Cervantes: Named after the famous writer Miguel de Cervantes, this serene park offers beautifully landscaped gardens, winding paths, and a tranquil pond where you can spot ducks and turtles.

Finca Güell: Get a taste of Antoni Gaudí's genius at the lesser-known Finca Güell. This architectural gem showcases Gaudí's distinctive style and provides an opportunity to appreciate his innovative designs up close.

Can Deu: Delve into the local culture at Can Deu, a historic building transformed into a vibrant cultural center. With art exhibitions, concerts, and other events, it's a hub for creativity and a platform for local talent.

Hidden Gems in Les Corts

Les Corts might not be known for its hidden gems, but there are a few delightful surprises waiting to be uncovered. Here are a couple of hidden gems that add a special touch to the district:

- **Parc de la Maternitat**: Escape the city chaos and discover the tranquility of Parc de la Maternitat. This hidden oasis in Les Corts offers peaceful gardens, shaded paths, and a serene pond. It's the perfect hideaway to relax, unwind, and enjoy a picnic away from the crowds.
- **Mercat de Les Corts**: Immerse yourself in the local culture at Mercat de Les Corts, a traditional food

market. Wander through the bustling stalls filled with fresh produce, tasty treats, and aromatic spices. Engage in friendly conversations with the vendors and get a taste of the vibrant culinary scene in Barcelona.

- **Casa Comalat**: Prepare to be amazed by Casa Comalat, a hidden architectural gem designed by the talented modernist architect Salvador Valeri i Pupurull. This unique building stands out with its intricate details and captivating features, making it a true standout in the neighborhood. Take a leisurely stroll and let its beauty captivate you.

Remember, sometimes the best hidden gems are found by simply following your curiosity, exploring the local streets, and embracing the unexpected.

Sarrià-Sant Gervasi

Located in the foothills of the Collserola mountain range, known for its upscale residential areas.

If you're exploring Sarrià-Sant Gervasi, here are some popular attractions to check out:

Parc de Collserola: This massive natural park on the outskirts of Barcelona is perfect for nature lovers. You can enjoy picturesque hiking trails, stunning viewpoints, and a peaceful retreat away from the city's hustle and bustle.

CosmoCaixa: A fantastic science museum that's sure to captivate both kids and adults. It features interactive exhibits,

211

a fascinating planetarium, and even an indoor rainforest. Get ready to have a blast while learning about science!

Plaça de Sarrià: This charming square serves as the vibrant heart of the Sarrià neighborhood. It's a great place to relax at an outdoor café, soak in the local atmosphere, and perhaps indulge in some people-watching.

Carrer Major de Sarrià: Take a leisurely stroll along this picturesque street in Sarrià. You'll encounter historic buildings, delightful local shops, and beautiful traditional architecture that adds to the area's charm.

Casa Roviralta: A hidden gem of modernist architecture, designed by the talented Joan Rubió i Bellver. This unique building showcases the artistic flair of the Art Nouveau style, and it's a treat for the eyes

Please check the opening hours and any specific guidelines for these attractions before you visit, as things may change. Enjoy exploring Sarrià-Sant Gervasi and discovering its delightful treasures!

Hidden Gems in Sarrià-Sant Gervasi

- **Carrer de Los Vergós**: Picture a charming, narrow street with lovely houses and local boutiques. Carrer de Los Vergós has that cozy, village-like vibe perfect for a leisurely stroll or some casual window shopping.
- **El Turó del Putxet**: This secret hill offers a hidden park where you can enjoy stunning panoramic views of Barcelona. It's an ideal spot to escape the crowds,

pack a picnic, and relax while taking in the breathtaking scenery.

- **Casa de l'Oli**: Calling all olive oil enthusiasts! This gem of a shop and tasting room showcases the finest Catalan olive oils. Learn about the different varieties, their production process, and savor some delectable oils that will take your taste buds on an adventure.

- **Galvany Market**: If you want to experience a more local vibe, head to the Galvany Market. It's a bustling market with an array of fresh produce, gourmet goodies, and local delicacies. You'll feel like a true insider as you explore the authentic market culture.

- **Plaça Artós**: Imagine a picturesque square surrounded by charming buildings and cozy cafés. Plaça Artós is the place to be for a relaxing coffee break or a moment of tranquility while soaking up the neighborhood's inviting atmosphere.

- **Sarrià Cemetery**: While it may seem unusual to visit a cemetery, Sarrià Cemetery has its own unique charm. It's a peaceful place with beautiful architecture, sculptures, and an ambiance of serenity. Take a stroll through history and find solace in its quiet beauty.

Gràcia

Gràcia, one of Barcelona's vibrant districts, has a distinctive bohemian vibe, an independent spirit, and a collection of

213

charming streets. It's a neighborhood where you'll find an array of unique shops, cozy bars, enticing restaurants, and cultural hotspots.

Let's explore some of the top tourist attractions in Gràcia:

- **Parc Güell**: A true gem and a UNESCO World Heritage Site, Parc Güell is a masterpiece by Antoni Gaudí. The park is a whimsical wonderland filled with vibrant mosaics, enchanting sculptures, and breathtaking views of the city.

- **Casa Vicens:** Designed by Gaudí back in 1883, Casa Vicens is a stunning Art Nouveau mansion. The intricate details and architectural finesse make it an important testament to Gaudí's early genius.

- **Plaça del Sol**: The pulsating heart of Gràcia, Plaça del Sol is a bustling square that attracts both locals and visitors. With its eclectic mix of shops, cozy cafes, and lively restaurants, there's always something happening here, from street performances to spontaneous dance parties.

- **Plaça de la Vila de Gràcia**: This charming square is home to the Gràcia Town Hall and serves as a focal point for events and festivals. It's an ideal spot to immerse yourself in the neighborhood's lively atmosphere and observe the vibrant local scene.

- **Mercat de la Llibertat**: If you want to experience the essence of local life, head to Mercat de la Llibertat. This vibrant market offers an abundance of fresh produce, delightful meats, tantalizing cheeses, and other local goodies. It's not just a place to shop, but also an opportunity to soak up the lively ambiance and witness the authentic local culture.

Hidden Gems in Gràcia

There's so much more to explore in Gràcia beyond the popular attractions! Let me share some other places you can visit and a few hidden gems waiting to be discovered:

- **Casa Fuster:** Check out this incredible modernist building, now transformed into a luxurious hotel. Marvel at its stunning architecture from the outside or treat yourself to a fabulous meal or a refreshing drink at one of its elegant establishments.

- **Mercat de l'Abaceria Central**: For a genuine local market experience, head to Mercat de l'Abaceria Central. It's a hidden gem, less crowded than the touristy markets, where you can find fresh produce, artisanal products, and tasty treats.

- **Plaça de la Virreina**: Picture a charming square with a lovely fountain and a lively atmosphere. Take a break, sip a coffee, and simply enjoy the vibrant ambiance. Don't forget to visit the beautiful Church of Sant Joan nearby.

- **Casa Ramos**: You won't want to miss this hidden treasure of modernist architecture tucked away on Carrer Gran de Gràcia. Take a moment to appreciate its intricate details and sculptural elements if you're a fan of architectural beauty.

- **Plaça del Diamant**: Known as the "Square of the Little Birds," this enchanting square is famous for its association with Mercè Rodoreda's novel, "La plaça del Diamant." It's a charming spot to relax, surrounded by cozy cafes and quaint shops.
- **Filmoteca de Catalunya**: Movie buffs, rejoice! This hidden gem is a cinema dedicated to screening a diverse range of classic and contemporary films. Check their schedule and catch a unique cinematic experience in a cozy setting.
- **Plaça Rius i Taulet**: This vibrant square is a hub of cultural events, concerts, and festivals. Join the locals as they gather to socialize, enjoy live music, and soak up the lively atmosphere.

Horta-Guinardó

Situated in the northeastern part of the city, it includes the beautiful Park Güell.

Horta-Guinardó, the city's third largest district, sprawls across the valleys and slopes of the Serra de Collserola foothills. It has some fantastic attractions that are worth exploring. Let's take a look at them:

- **Recinte Modernista de Sant Pau:** This architectural gem was once a hospital complex designed by Lluis Domenech i Montaner back in 1902. It's a sight to behold and offers a fascinating glimpse into the city's history.

- **The Carmel Bunkers:** Get ready to step back in time at this historic site. It provides a lookout point where you can soak up amazing views of Barcelona while learning about its past.

- **Parque del Laberint d'Horta:** Get lost in the magic of this park. With its enchanting maze, tranquil vistas, and refreshing shaded pathways, it's a wonderful place to unwind and enjoy a leisurely stroll.

- **Gaudi House Museum:** Calling all Gaudí fans! This museum, located inside Guel Park, is a treasure trove of Gaudí's artistry. Explore the house where he once resided and immerse yourself in his fascinating world.

- **Montserrat:** Don't forget to check out this impressive monument/statue in Montbau. The journey to the monastery offers breathtaking views that are well worth the visit.

- **Parc del Guinardó:** With a convenient parking lot at its base and picturesque paths to wander, it's an ideal spot to take a breather and enjoy the surrounding greenery.

Hidden Gems in Horta-Guinardó

Els Tres Turons Park: This park is a hidden paradise offering several lookout points that provide stunning views of the city and the glistening Mediterranean Sea. The most famous of these viewpoints is the **Turó de la Rovira**, where you can stand on the remains of former anti-aircraft batteries from the Spanish Civil War and soak in the incredible vistas.

Another hidden gem is the **Labyrinth Park**, the oldest park in the city. Created back in 1791, it boasts a Neo-classical garden featuring a serene pond and, of course, a labyrinth made of cypress-tree hedges. Instead of a Minotaur, you'll find a statue of Eros, the Greek god of love, at its center. It's a unique and romantic spot to explore.

For a taste of Horta's history, take a stroll along **Carrer d'Aiguafreda** in the Horta neighborhood. This street still bears remnants of its thriving clothes washing industry from the 19th century. It's a fascinating glimpse into the district's past.

To experience the charm of Horta's old town, make your way to **Plaça d'Eivissa** and its surroundings. Here, the original structure and essence of Horta's former village have been lovingly preserved. It's a delightful area to wander around and soak up the quaint atmosphere.

Nou Barris

A working-class district in the northern part of Barcelona, characterized by its diverse communities.

Let's talk about Nou Barris, a district located in the northwestern part of Barcelona, Spain. It's a residential area comprising 14 neighborhoods and is known for its authentic charm. Nou Barris is a haven of parks and gardens, making it a delightful place to explore.

Top Attractions

- **Escape Barcelona**: Get ready for an exhilarating adventure at this escape game venue. Test your wits, solve puzzles, and try to escape within the given time limit. It's a fun and challenging experience for puzzle enthusiasts.

- **Castillo De Torre Baró**: Feel like a royal as you visit this captivating castle and point of interest. Explore its grounds, soak up the historical ambiance, and imagine yourself in a bygone era.

- **Parc Central de Nou Barris**: This architectural building and bridge are definitely eye-catching. Take a stroll, appreciate the unique design, and enjoy the green surroundings. It's a perfect spot for a leisurely walk or a peaceful picnic.

- **El Corte Ingles Can Drago**: Shopaholics, rejoice! This department store offers a variety of shopping options. Browse through the latest fashion trends, discover local brands, or treat yourself to something special.

- **Fundacio Brafa**: Let your little ones have a blast at this playground. It's a great place for kids to burn off some energy, enjoy the slides and swings, and have fun in a safe and playful environment.

- **SOM Multiespai**: Need to satisfy your shopping cravings? Head to this shopping mall where you can find a range of stores, boutiques, and eateries. It's a one-stop destination for all your retail needs.
- **Jardins de Llucmajor**: Take a break from the bustling city and unwind in this lovely park and garden. Enjoy the serene surroundings, take a leisurely stroll, and embrace the natural beauty around you.
- **MUHBA Casa de l'Aigua**: Dive into history at this specialty museum. Learn about the significance of water and its role in Barcelona's past through interactive exhibits and displays.

Hidden Gems

Among the hidden gems waiting to be discovered in Nou Barris is **Plaça de ca N'Enseya**. This modern park spans a whopping 17 hectares, making it the second largest park in the city. Within its vast expanse, you'll find notable structures such as the transformed **Santa Creu Mental Institution**, which now serves as a library, and the Nou Barris Council Headquarters. It's a unique and picturesque spot worth checking out.

Another hidden gem worth mentioning is the enchanting **Turó de la Peira** park and the lovely **Guineueta Park**. Both offer tranquil retreats where you can immerse yourself in nature, relax, and recharge.

If you have an appreciation for sculptures, make sure to visit **Plaça Llucmajor**. Here, you'll find captivating sculptures created by Francesc Pi i Margall. They add an artistic touch to the square and provide an opportunity to admire the creativity of this talented artist.

Sant Andreu

A traditional and residential district with a village-like atmosphere.

The district takes its name from the former municipality of Sant Andreu de Palomar, which used to be the largest in the area and now forms the core of the neighborhood that bears its name. What makes Sant Andreu special is its local and traditional ambiance, having once been a separate village before merging with Barcelona back in 1897.

Now, let's explore some of the top attractions that Sant Andreu has to offer. One notable gem is the **Sant Andreu church**. Unlike many of the iconic Gothic churches in the city, this one stands out with its impressive dome, a departure from the usual spires. It's fascinating to discover that this church was built on the site of a 10th-century Romanesque church, adding a layer of historical richness to its architectural charm.

Another attraction worth visiting is **Fabra i Coats**, a former factory that has been transformed into a vibrant arts and cultural center. Here, you'll find artist workshops, captivating exhibitions, lively concerts, and a hub of artistic activities. It's a dynamic space that embraces creativity and offers a unique experience for art enthusiasts.

Sant Andreu embodies the essence of local life, preserving its own distinct character while being a part of the bustling city of Barcelona.

Top Attractions

La Maquinista: Get your shopping fix at this lively shopping mall. Browse through a variety of stores, enjoy delicious meals at the food court, and discover the latest trends in fashion and more.

Enigma - Escape Room Barcelona: If you're up for a thrilling challenge, head to this escape game venue. Test your problem-solving skills, unravel mysteries, and try to escape within the given time. It's a fantastic activity for those seeking an adrenaline rush.

Gimnasio Puro Impacto Barcelona: This sports complex offers a range of fitness facilities and activities to keep you active. Whether you're into boxing, cardio, or weightlifting, you'll find something to suit your fitness goals.

Museo Alien: Step into the realm of extraterrestrial wonders at this specialty museum. Explore exhibits dedicated to aliens, UFOs, and otherworldly phenomena. It's a unique and captivating experience for those intrigued by the unknown.

Whitechapel Room Escape: Another fantastic escape game venue where you can test your skills and teamwork. Dive into immersive scenarios, solve puzzles, and race against the clock to escape. It's a thrilling adventure for friends and family.

Parc de la Trinitat: Need some fresh air and green surroundings? Look no further than this park. Enjoy leisurely walks, relax in the tranquil ambiance, and maybe even have a picnic. It's a great spot to unwind and connect with nature.

Fugitivos Room Escape: Engage your mind and have a blast at this escape game venue. Challenge yourself with mind-boggling puzzles, work together with your team, and see if you can break free before time runs out.

Parque de la Pegaso: Another lovely park to explore in Sant Andreu. Take a break, enjoy a leisurely stroll, and appreciate the natural beauty of the surroundings. It's a peaceful retreat away from the hustle and bustle.

Esglesia de Sant Andreu de Palomar: Don't miss the opportunity to visit this impressive church and cathedral. Marvel at its architectural beauty, soak in the serene ambiance, and appreciate the historical significance of this religious landmark.

MUHBA at Fabra i Coats: Immerse yourself in history at this specialty museum. Discover the stories and artifacts that showcase Barcelona's past and its cultural heritage. It's a fascinating journey through time.

Hidden Gems in Sant Andreu

- One of these hidden gems is **Fabra i Coats**. This former factory has been transformed into a bustling arts and cultural center. Inside, you'll find artist workshops buzzing with creativity and a vibrant space that hosts fascinating exhibitions, lively concerts, and artistic activities. But here's the exciting part: during Christmas time, the factory turns into the toy workshop of The Three Kings! Kids from all over Barcelona flock here for a chance to meet one of the Kings, share their Christmas wishlist, and even receive a small gift. It's a magical experience that brings joy to young hearts.

- **Sant Pacià church**. Tucked away and little-known, this 19th-century Neo-Gothic church holds a remarkable secret. Inside, you'll find some of architect Antoni Gaudí's work. Marvel at the intricately designed floor mosaics, admire the unique lamps, and take in the beauty of the altar. The best part is that this church is hardly visited by tourists, so you'll have the privilege of experiencing its charm in serene solitude.

Sant Marti

Home to the iconic beaches of Barcelona, it has seen significant urban renewal in recent years.

It's a diverse district that shares borders with the Mediterranean Sea, Sant Adrià del Besòs, and four other vibrant districts of Barcelona: Ciutat Vella, l'Eixample, Horta-Guinardó, and Sant Andreu[1]. The district takes its name from the iconic Saint Martin church and is home to a population of approximately 221,029 people, making it the second most populated district in Barcelona. With an area of

10.8 km², it ranks as the fourth largest district and has a population density of around 20,466 inhabitants per square kilometer[1].

Now, let's explore the ten neighborhoods that make up Sant Martí:

1. El Besòs i el Maresme: This neighborhood encompasses the areas along the Besòs River and the coastal Maresme area.

2. El Camp de l'Arpa del Clot: Known for its vibrant atmosphere, this neighborhood offers a mix of residential and commercial areas.

3. El Clot: This neighborhood is home to the iconic Clot Market and exudes a lively charm with its bustling streets.

4. Diagonal Mar i Front Marítim del Poblenou: Located along the iconic Diagonal Avenue, this neighborhood boasts a modern feel and offers a beautiful waterfront area.

5. El Parc i Llacuna del Poblenou: Nestled near the Poblenou Park, this neighborhood combines green spaces with residential areas.

6. El Poblenou: Once an industrial area, El Poblenou has transformed into a trendy neighborhood with a vibrant cultural scene.

7. Provençals del Poblenou: This neighborhood offers a mix of residential areas and commercial establishments, creating a lively local atmosphere.

8. Sant Martí de Provençals: Known for its community spirit, this neighborhood preserves its traditional charm.

9. La Verneda i la Pau: Located near the Besòs River, this neighborhood is known for its peaceful ambiance and green spaces.

10. La Vila Olímpica del Poblenou: As the name suggests, this neighborhood was built for the 1992 Olympic Games. It offers a stunning waterfront area and a vibrant atmosphere.

Top Attractions

El Parque de Sant Marti: This large community park is a hidden oasis. Picture a tranquil square nestled under the shade of dense trees, and it's made even more special by its unique construction process that took place over a span of ten years. Each distinct space within the park showcases the different stages of its creation. It's a serene escape where you can relax and immerse yourself in nature.

Diagonal Mar: If you're up for some retail therapy, head to this expansive shopping mall located in the Diagonal Mar i Front Marítim del Poblenou neighborhood. With a wide range of stores and boutiques, you can satisfy your shopping cravings and indulge in some leisurely browsing.

Bogatell Beach: Take a break from city life and bask in the sun at this popular beach in the Poblenou neighborhood. Enjoy the sandy shores, take a refreshing dip in the sea, and soak up the vibrant beach atmosphere.

El Poblenou: This neighborhood has a fascinating history as an industrial hub, but it has undergone a remarkable transformation into a vibrant center for art and creativity. Explore its charming streets, discover local art galleries, and witness the fusion of past and present.

Museu de Ciencies Naturals de Barcelona: Dive into the fascinating world of natural history and science at this museum located in the Forum area. Explore captivating exhibits, learn about the wonders of the natural world, and engage in interactive displays that spark curiosity.

Torre Agbar: Marvel at the striking architecture of this iconic skyscraper designed by French architect Jean Nouvel. The Torre Agbar has become a landmark of the city, with its unique shape and vibrant illuminations that light up the Barcelona skyline.

Port Olimpic: Experience the lively waterfront ambiance at Port Olimpic. This marina area offers an array of restaurants, bars, and a vibrant nightlife scene. Enjoy a delicious meal, sip cocktails by the waterfront, and soak up the energetic atmosphere.

Rambla del Poblenou: Stroll along this charming tree-lined avenue that captures the essence of Sant Martí. It's adorned with shops, cozy cafes, and enticing restaurants. Take a leisurely walk, grab a cup of coffee, and immerse yourself in the local vibe.

Hidden Gems in Sant Marti

Conclusion

Well, folks, we've reached the end of our Barcelona tourist guidebook journey. We hope you've enjoyed the ride as much as we have!

From strolling along the Gothic Quarter's narrow streets to basking in the Mediterranean sun on Barceloneta Beach, we've shared some of the city's most delightful secrets. And, let's not forget the endless supply of mouth-watering tapas, refreshing Sangria, and velvety cappuccinos that we've indulged in along the way.

But, before we bid adiós, let us leave you with this question - ¿Cómo no amar a Barcelona? (How can you not love Barcelona?) From the vibrancy of the city to the warmth of the people, Barcelona truly is a gem of the Mediterranean.

So, whether you're soaking in the stunning views of Park Guell, admiring the whimsical designs of Gaudi or simply taking a stroll through the lively Ramblas, we hope you'll take a little piece of Barcelona back home with you.

Thank you for joining us on this unforgettable adventure. May your travels continue to be filled with joy, wonder, and endless adventures. ¡Hasta pronto! (See you soon!)

Printed in Great Britain
by Amazon